CANAL WALKS

SOUTH

RAY QUINLAN

ALAN SUTTON

To Mum and Dad
who have never had
a book
dedicated to them
before.

First published in the United Kingdom in 1992 by
Alan Sutton Publishing Ltd · Phoenix Mill · Stroud · Gloucestershire

Reprinted 1994

British Library Cataloguing in Publication Data

Quinlan, Ray
  Canal Walks: South
  I. Title
  914.204

  ISBN 0-86299-994-4

Library of Congress Cataloging in Publication Data applied for

Typeset in 10/12 Plantin.
Typesetting and origination by
Alan Sutton Publishing Limited.
Printed and bound in Great Britain by
WBC, Bridgend, Mid Glam.

CONTENTS

ACKNOWLEDGEMENTS   iv

LOCATION OF WALKS   v

KEY TO MAPS   vi

INTRODUCTION   vii

1   The Basingstoke Canal   1

2   The Brecon & Abergavenny Canal   15

3   The Bridgwater & Taunton Canal   29

4   The Bude Canal   43

5   The Chelmer & Blackwater Navigation   56

6   The Grand Junction Canal   68

7   The Kennet & Avon Canal   84

8   The Oxford Canal   100

9   The Regent's Canal   116

10   The Royal Military Canal   130

11   The Thames & Severn Canal   145

12   The Wey & Arun Junction Canal   161

APPENDIX A   General Reading   177

APPENDIX B   Useful Addresses   178

APPENDIX C   Museums   179

INDEX   181

ACKNOWLEDGEMENTS

This book would have been impossible without the splendid resources of various libraries: communal ownership in practice. Despite chronic under-funding, the information and help received was substantial.

Help and advice on the routes came from: Mrs Audrey Wheatley of the Bude Canal Society; W.J. Spall of the Chelmer & Blackwater Navigation Ltd; staff of the National Rivers Authority; David Jowett of the Cotswolds Canals Trust; Brian Forder of the Monmouthshire, Brecon & Abergavenny Canals Trust Ltd; and John Wood of the Wey & Arun Canal Trust. Thanks also to the various employees of British Waterways who, as ever, have been both helpful and cooperative.

Assistance with archive photographs came from Roy Jamieson of British Waterways; Lynn Doylerush of the Boat Museum; Ms J.T. Smith of Essex Record Office; R. Bowder of Marylebone Library; Victoria Williams of Hastings Museum; Mr P.A.L. Vine; and the staff of the National Monuments Record. Thanks also to members of the Sussex Archaeological Trust. Assistance with, though no responsibility for, the author's pictures came from Mr Ilford and Mr Fuji and two old and steadily deteriorating Olympuses fitted with 28 mm and 75–150 mm lenses.

For assistance during walking trips, thanks go to Mike and Val of Berry Park, Welcombe, and to Kath (who also helped with some inter-library loans!). Thanks also to Tessa and Miles for helping me with at least one 'two-car trick'. As before, much appreciation to Taffy for most of the trans-portation. And, of course, thanks to Mary who continued to provide her wonderful support throughout.

LOCATION OF WALKS

1. Basingstoke Canal at Woking
2. Brecon & Abergavenny Canal at Brecon
3. Bridgwater & Taunton Canal at Taunton
4. Bude Canal at Bude
5. Chelmer & Blackwater Navigation at Heybridge
6. Grand Junction Canal at Tring
7. Kennet & Avon Canal at Bradford-on-Avon
8. Oxford Canal at Oxford
9. Regent's Canal at Camden
10. Royal Military Canal at Rye
11. Thames & Severn Canal in the Golden Valley
12. Wey & Arun Junction Canal at Loxwood

KEY TO MAPS

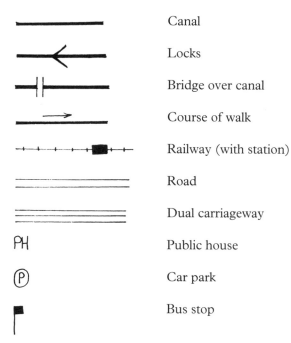

Canal

Locks

Bridge over canal

Course of walk

Railway (with station)

Road

Dual carriageway

PH   Public house

℗   Car park

Bus stop

INTRODUCTION

On a warm, sunny Friday in May 1991, a crowd of enthusiasts at Frimley Lodge Park, near Aldershot, cheered and waved as the Duke of Kent proclaimed the Basingstoke Canal officially re-opened. The canal, from its junction with the River Wey near Byfleet in Surrey to the closed tunnel at Greywell in Hampshire, was once thought to have been lost in a mass of scrubby vegetation, old mattresses and discarded supermarket trolleys. The commitment of 2,000 local canal society members and the vision of two county councils has turned a public embarrassment into a magnificent amenity. The Basingstoke Canal of the 1960s bears no resemblance to that of the 1990s. The 30 or so miles of restored waterway are now the pride of the area and a great attraction to boaters, naturalists, anglers and walkers alike. The Basingstoke is a modern-day success story and it typifies the change in attitude towards the nation's canals. Whereas twenty to thirty years ago they were objects of derision, now we all, it seems, appreciate them for the fine resource that they are.

Although many of the country's waterways have been restored in this way, only recently has their value for walking been fully appreciated. Even though British Waterways produces leaflets which proudly proclaim that it owns 1,500 miles of walking (more, as it puts it, than the Pennine Way and the Offa's Dyke Path put together), to date towpath walkers have mostly been tolerated rather than encouraged. Now, apparently, things are to change. The publication of this book coincides with British Waterways' announcement of the first National Waterway Walk (a title designed to be equivalent to a National Trail, like the aforementioned Pennine Way and Offa's Dyke). To commemorate the two-hundredth anniversary of canal mania, the 140 miles from the Gas Street Basin in central Birmingham along the Grand Union Canal to Paddington in London are set to become the bee's knees of canal walking. The towpath is to be upgraded to render it usable by the less able-bodied; there is to be better access; waymarks and information notices are to be erected; and, in that ultimate accolade which tells us that it's all kosher, there is to be an official walking guide.

Is this the answer to all those critics who say that towpaths are an ignored and abused resource? Well, nearly. The route will never be directly equivalent to a National Trail. National Trails are public rights of way on which walkers have the legal right of access at all times. British Waterways, however, is very firm that it will preserve its rights over the towpath. Unless they are already so dedicated, British Waterways' towpaths will not become public rights of way. British Waterways will retain the privilege of being able to withdraw access just as quickly as it gave it.

It is, of course, easy to carp. After all, on non-British Waterways canals (in this volume the Basingstoke, the Bude, the Chelmer & Blackwater, the Royal Military, the Thames & Severn and the Wey & Arun are all non-British Waterways-owned canals), walkers are restricted to public rights of way only and many miles remain closed. The establishment of the National Waterway Walk is therefore a great first step to the full appreciation of the nation's canals as long-distance walking routes. The Kennet & Avon is already acknowledged as one (if not officially). The Staffordshire & Worcestershire would make a splendid one if only some of the towpath was restored, and the Leeds & Liverpool could be become a fine, relatively flat, alternative to Wainwright's Coast to Coast. All towpathers should therefore welcome this move by British Waterways and encourage it to do more of the same. Furthermore, we might encourage them to convert all the nation's towpaths into the public rights of way that they should surely be.

The Southern Canals

At first glance, the southern canals appear to have less to offer than their Midlands counterparts. How can any line have the richness of history and scenery of a Staffordshire & Worcestershire or a Trent & Mersey? Yet there's no busier canal in the country than the Grand Junction and few lines anywhere share the variety of the Kennet & Avon. And none, simply none, can compare with the wonderful mountain setting of the Brecon & Abergavenny.

Mostly, however, the South's canals take on a much more somnolent air. The Basingstoke is the archetypal green finger through the suburbs of Surrey, and the Bridgwater & Taunton is so peaceful it almost snoozes its way between the two Somerset towns. The Chelmer & Blackwater is undoubtedly the acceptable face of Essex Man, while the Oxford Canal, despite the constant fear of finding one of Morse's corpses, is nothing short of a rural retreat. Even in their most urban form, and the Regent's Canal through central London cannot be more so, the southern canals have plenty to offer the towpather.

It must also be said that some of the South's canals have become so rural that they've all but disappeared into the undergrowth. The Kennet & Avon and the Basingstoke have only just survived to be re-opened within the last 2–3 years. Others, such as the Wey & Arun, the Thames & Severn and the

Bude, are in various states of disrepair and still have a somewhat doubtful future. And finally, what can be said of that most peculiar of defensive fortifications, the Royal Military Canal? Is it a canal? Is it a drainage ditch? Or is it simply a super place for an afternoon stroll?

Here is just a selection of the canals of the South and, although by no means arbitrary, it is strictly a personal choice. Walkers should not ignore the fine Wey Navigation (through Guildford), the Lee & Stort, the Gloucester & Sharpness, or the long-lost lines such as the Wiltshire & Berkshire, the Gloucester & Hereford, the Somerset Coal Canal, the Grand Western or the many other small canals of south Wales or south-west England. All these are worthy of further investigation and, with the aid of an Ordnance Survey map and some keen legs, can be traced both on paper and, often, on the ground.

As with all personal choices, some people's favourite lines or stretches of waterway may have been omitted. There is also the problem of what is a southern canal. Both the Oxford and the Grand Junction canals go just as far north as the Stratford and yet the latter was included in *Canal Walks: Midlands*. Furthermore, what exactly constitutes a canal? Could it not be argued that the best waterway walk in the South is the Thames 'Navigation'? In all these matters, only the author is to blame. I have not tried to be a sage on these matters, merely a stimulus. Walking the canals of the South should be an adventure with plenty to see and discover for yourselves. And it is quite likely that you will see even more than I did and enjoy them every bit as much.

Walking the Towpaths

The walks in this book are all straightforward and require no special feats of strength or navigation. Towpath walks have two great virtues: they are mostly on the flat; and they have a ready-made, unmistakable course to follow. Getting lost should therefore, in theory at least, be relatively hard. The key problem with towpath walks is that if you want to spend most of the day by the canal, circular routes to and from a vehicle or a particular station or bus-stop become difficult. Many of the walks in this volume involve walking one way and returning by public transport. This means that you must check the availability of the bus or train before travelling. Telephone numbers are provided and your local library should have the main British Rail timetable.

Walkers should generally plan for 2 to $2^1/2$ miles an hour so that stops can be made for sightseeing or a break. Head-down speedsters should easily manage three miles an hour on a good track. You should, of course, add a little time for stoppages for refreshment and add a lot of time if you are accompanied by photographers or bird-watchers.

No special equipment or provisions are needed to walk the towpaths of Britain. On a good day and on a good path, any comfortable footwear and clothing will do, and you'll be able to leave the laden rucksack at home. However, for longer walks through more remote country you should be more prudent. Even in a drought, towpaths can be extremely muddy and, from experience, it can not only rain virtually any time but usually does. Boots and a raincoat of some sort are therefore advisable. Similarly, although pubs and small shops are often fairly common along the way, it may be useful to carry some kind of snack and drink with you.

This book includes sketch maps that show the route to be taken. However, the local Ordnance Survey map will always be useful and the appropriate map numbers and references are provided in each chapter. Again, your local library may well have them for loan.

Finally, the dangers inherent in walking along a waterway are often not fully appreciated. Over the 1990 Christmas holiday, three children died after falling into a lock on the Kennet & Avon at Burghfield. A year later their mother committed suicide, having been unable to endure her loss. Locks are deep, often have silt-laden bottoms, and are very difficult to get out of. Everybody, especially children, should be made aware of this. If somebody does fall in, you should not go into the water except as a last resort. You should LIE on the bank and use something like a coat for the person to grab so that you can then pull them in. Better still, keep children away from the edge.

Otherwise, please enjoy.

1
THE BASINGSTOKE CANAL
West Byfleet to Ash Vale

Introduction

The commuter-land of north-west Surrey is an unpromising area for a canal, let alone an agricultural one, but herein lies a gem. Although it's often given the somewhat over-used epithet of 'green finger', the Basingstoke Canal is as close as you'll come to such a thing.

Starting where the London-Southampton railway and the M25 compete for attention at West Byfleet, the canal leaves the River Wey to follow a leafy course through Woking, Brookwood and Frimley before entering Hampshire at Aldershot. After skirting Farnborough airfield, the line goes through Fleet and on to the villages of Crookham and Odiham. Contrary to expectations, the current route of the Basingstoke Canal does not go to Basingstoke. Instead it stops 4 miles to the east at one of the most notorious sites in canal restoration: the Greywell Tunnel. Boat enthusiasts argue in favour of re-opening the tunnel which was closed in 1932. However, the cave-like interior is an important roosting site for that most beleaguered of animals, the bat. Nature lovers, including English Nature, argue that restoration would disturb the bats in one of their last major refuges in this part of the country. At the time of writing, the debate continues and the tunnel remains closed, a situation no doubt welcomed by the bats. Whatever the arguments, it is true that re-opening the tunnel would not add much to the navigable length of the waterway. Beyond Greywell Hill, the canal runs for just another mile before coming to a complete stop. Although it is still possible to trace the course of the line into central Basingstoke, beyond Up Nately the land has been sold and a lot of it redeveloped.

Despite all of this, the Basingstoke is a breath of fresh air for the area and justifiably a popular spot. But if you take your wildlife identification guides with you, it may be tactful to keep them hidden from passing boaters!

History

Whereas most canal sponsors saw their main source of revenue in the shipment of minerals, coal or manufactured goods, the prime purpose of the investors of north Hampshire was to give a boost to the local farming community. They believed that the benefits of the canal would be seen through the cheap importation of fertilizer and in the reduced cost of shipping produce to the great markets in London.

The first scheme to link Basingstoke with the Thames (and hence London) was suggested in 1770. Benjamin Davis, who surveyed the route, planned to follow the Loddon Valley as far as Twyford and then to bear east via White Waltham to Monkey Island near Bray on the Thames. This proposal was later changed to a route from Basingstoke to the navigable River Wey at Byfleet and was surveyed for a group of enthusiastic investors by Joseph Parker in 1776. The sponsors of the canal claimed that it would 'furnish timber for the Navy' (a politically expedient claim at the time) 'and also supply the London markets with flour and grain at a cheaper rate' (politically expedient at any time). Parliament was obviously convinced by the argument. An Act authorizing the route and providing the powers to raise £86,000 (with £40,000 more if necessary) followed in 1778. This was despite opposition from the people of Reading who feared loss of their country trade to the new, possibly quicker, route to London.

Parker's surveyed course broadly followed the route we see today. The only significant difference occurs between Odiham and Basingstoke. Here Parker proposed a 6 mile loop to Turgis Green. This idea was dropped following the protestations of the local landowner, Lord Tylney, who felt that he was being encircled by the waterway. As a result, the Greywell Tunnel was built. This cut the total length of the canal from the original 44 miles to the built 37½. The tunnel had the additional benefit of tapping an underground water source and remains to this day an important supply, with the long summit pound from Aldershot to Greywell acting as a kind of linear reservoir for the rest of the canal.

The uncertainty caused by the American War of Independence delayed construction work and it wasn't until 1788 that the Basingstoke Canal Navigation Company appointed William Jessop as engineer. He promptly carried out the final survey, engaged John Pinkerton as contractor and building work began. The first tolls were collected in 1791 and by August 1792 some 32 miles (from the Wey to Greywell), including twenty-four locks, were navigable. However, the cost involved in doing so meant that a new Act was needed in 1793 to raise a further £60,000. Greywell Tunnel was finally ready and the entire length (37½ miles and twenty-nine locks) opened on 4 September 1794. The canal could handle barges 82^1/$_2$ ft long by 14^1/$_2$ ft wide, each carrying 50 ton loads and able to travel the 71 miles from London to Basingstoke in three or four days. In the early years, barges to London carried malt, flour and timber, while those from London carried coal and groceries.

To cope with the expected rush, company wharves were built at Horsell, Frimley, Ash, Farnham Road (west Aldershot), Crookham, Winchfield, Odiham, Basing and Basingstoke. The company also maintained its own fleet of boats. At Basingstoke, road transport was available to carry goods on to Winchester and Southampton. Later, it was hoped, the Itchen Navigation, which ran from Southampton to Winchester, would be extended so that a continuous water line from London to Salisbury and Southampton would be available. Sadly, this hope was not to be fulfilled and the canal was never a financial success. With a cost of about £153,000 (against the original estimate of £87,000), the line was always in debt and the company found it hard to keep up the payments of its loan interest, a factor which added a further £37,000 to the overall bill. As a result, the shareholders never received a dividend. The reason for the failure was that the canal was simply not as busy as forecast. Whereas the company had predicted business of 30,700 tons p.a. carried for 5s. per ton, the actual figures were considerably lower. In 1801–2, for example, 18,737 tons were carried at about 4s. per ton. Thus, the predicted annual revenue of £7,783 was never realized and annual income was usually around £2,000. The end of the war with France in 1815 didn't help. A lot of traffic from the Isle of Wight and the Channel Islands, which formerly used the inland route, could now risk the sea passage to London and did so, as it was both quicker and cheaper. By 1818, the canal also faced competition from road transport which, although marginally more expensive, was both faster and more direct.

Undoubtedly the key disadvantage of the canal was that it stopped at Basingstoke. Although proposals were made to take the line to Southampton, the company could never raise either interest or funds to build the extension. One scheme, proposed in 1807, was the Portsmouth, Southampton & London Junction Canal, which would have linked the Grand Surrey Canal (which joined the Thames at Rotherhithe) with the Basingstoke and (via Aldershot, Farnham and Winchester) the Itchen Navigation. This idea floundered on an unfavourable report from John Rennie and opposition from land and mill owners. A link with the Kennet & Avon to produce an alternative London–Bristol route was proposed in 1825 but never started. The Hampshire & Berkshire Junction Canal, as it was called, would have linked Basing, a village to the east of Basingstoke, to Newbury. The proposal was opposed by the Thames Commissioners who were successful in having the idea scrapped despite the enthusiasm (and the cash) of both the Basingstoke and K&A companies.

When the London & Southampton Railway (later renamed the London & South Western) was built, the decline was almost complete. Ironically, things improved slightly while the new railway was under construction as the canal was used to ship building materials for the new line. But in June 1839 the railway reached Basingstoke and in May 1840 it was open all the way to Southampton. The end of the canal as a going concern was inevitable. In the first year after the railway opened, canal toll receipts fell by 30 per cent. Business improved when the army camp at Aldershot was being built in the 1850s, but by 1865 income had dropped by nearly 80 per cent. As a result, the company went into liquidation in 1866.

There now followed a series of speculative and dubious financial deals:

1866   Original company liquidated – in hands of receiver
1874   William St Aubyn forms the Surrey & Hants Canal Company
1878   Canal in hands of receiver
1880   Canal bought by Messrs Dixon & Ward (for £14,800)
1880   Canal bought by J.B. Smith
1880   Surrey & Hampshire Canal Corporation formed nominally to sell water to London but more probably as a way of extracting funds from foolhardy investors
1882   Canal in hands of receiver
1883   London & Hampshire Canal & Water Company formed by some of the creditors of the Surrey & Hants
1887   Canal in hands of receiver
1895   Canal bought by Sir Frederick Hunt
1896   Woking, Aldershot & Basingstoke Canal and Navigation Company formed
1900   Canal in hands of receiver
1905   Canal bought by William Carter and sold to Horatio Bottomley's Joint Stock Trust & Finance Corporation
1908   London & South-Western Canal Company formed which again successfully invited investors to make the proprietors rich
1909   Canal rebought by William Carter
1914   Basingstoke Canal Syndicate bought the canal for £15,000
1921   Canal in hands of receiver and bought by William Carter
1923   Canal bought by A.J. Harmsworth
1937   Weybridge, Woking & Aldershot Canal Company formed by Harmsworth
1949   Canal in hands of receiver
1950   Canal bought for £6,000 by the New Basingstoke Canal Company

Despite the many dubious business transactions and the numerous name changes, by 1901 commercial traffic on the canal had virtually stopped after

A.J. Harmsworth, standing on the cabin of *Basingstoke*, attempts to pass through the canal near Up Nately in late 1913. This, the last attempt to go along the entire canal, was not successful but did enable the line to be kept open as a commercial concern

British Waterways

the brickworks at Up Nately had closed. In 1913, Alec Harmsworth took the narrow boat *Basingstoke* along the whole length of the canal in order to prove that it could still be done. It took three months. The First World War revived fortunes, but only temporarily, and for a while the canal was used as a reservoir. By 1923, when Alec Harmsworth bought the canal, there was no traffic west of Woking. The potentially disastrous collapse of Greywell Tunnel in 1932, which finally sealed the route to Basingstoke, therefore had no practical effect on trade. The years of Harmsworth's ownership, however, were good for the canal. Here at last was a man who was actually interested in the line as a working waterway. Because of the traffic to the gasworks at Woking, trade peaked in 1935 at 31,577 tons; a period of prosperity second only to that of 1838–9 when the railway was being built. This Indian summer came to an end in 1936 when the Woking District Gas Company ceased to make its own gas. After Harmsworth died in 1947, some timber traffic continued but on 15 March 1949 the final load was delivered to Spanton's Yard beside Chertsey Road, Woking. This was quickly followed by yet another company liquidation. By the 1960s the whole line was derelict, the locks inoperable and the canal itself mostly overgrown with weed or filled with rubbish and silt.

The revival of the Basingstoke Canal began in 1966 when a group of enthusiasts formed the Surrey & Hampshire Canal Society. Their first major success was in persuading the relevant county councils to recognize the value of the navigation as an amenity and to purchase it. The Hampshire stretch was bought in 1973 and the Surrey section in 1975. Since then, this consortium of interests, fronted by the Basingstoke Canal Authority, has dragged the canal back to health by clearing the waterway, repairing the locks and improving the towpath and other facilities. It has cost about £3–4 million. This effort was rewarded on 10 May 1991 when the Duke of Kent declared the line re-opened. Today, given adequate water, the entire length from the Wey through to Greywell is theoretically open to leisure cruising.

The Walk

Start: West Byfleet BR station (OS ref: SU 042611)
Finish: Ash Vale BR station (OS ref: SU 893534). Shorter routes stop at Woking or Brookwood
Distance: 14 miles/22^1/2 km (or 4 miles to Woking; 87 miles to Brookwood)
Maps: OS Landranger 186 (Aldershot & Guildford) plus 1/4 mile on 176
Return: BR Ash Vale to West Byfleet. Short walks return from Woking or Brookwood stations (enquiries: 0483-755905)
Car park: At West Byfleet station or by the canal off Camphill Road (OS ref: SU 046616). It is also possible to park at Ash Vale station
Public transport: The London to Southampton BR line at West Byfleet

The walk starts at West Byfleet station. There is a large car park to the east of the station which is free at weekends. From the station, turn left to a minor crossroads and then left along Madeira Road. At a T-junction, turn left along Camphill Road past a school and under a railway bridge. The road bends right and then left to reach a bridge (Scotland Bridge) over the canal. The main walk now turns left. However, if you wish to see the junction of the canal with the River Wey Navigation, turn right to go down this (southern) side, passing firstly some houseboats and then lock 1. Before long the M25 can be seen perched on stilts in the distance. This detour (including the return) is just over 1 mile.

The Wey Navigation runs from the Thames at Weybridge to Guildford

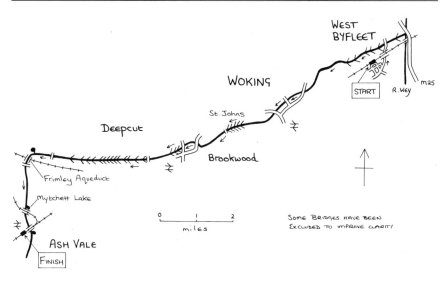

The Basingstoke Canal

and then on to Godalming. At one time it was possible to navigate from London to Portsmouth along this route (via the Wey & Arun Canal), but alas no longer. The junction here at Byfleet isn't spectacular scenery but offers the interesting sight of three ages of transport overlaying each other in a kind of concrete sandwich. The Wey Navigation of the mid-seventeenth century is bridged by the London and South-Western Railway of the mid-nineteenth century, which in turn is bridged by the M25 of the mid-twentieth. It is, of course, a matter of taste as to which is preferred.

From the Wey, return along the canal to Scotland Bridge. The main walk starts on the southern bank. From the bridge turn left so that the canal is on your right. Within a short distance you pass a group of locks (2–6) known as the Woodham Locks. It was this section of the canal that was started first and these locks were open in mid-1791. The first toll was collected from a boat carrying 'merchandise' to Horsell. Tolls were collected at the lock-house at lock 3. At the time of my visits, the pound between locks 4 and 5 was completely dry. Basingstoke Canal has no artificial water supply and relies entirely on natural springs, such as those in Greywell Tunnel, and the wash-off from roads, soil, etc. During periods of drought, therefore, levels can become very low, leading to the closure of the navigation.

After a road bridge, the towpath passes the last Woodham Lock and loops in between houses, some of which have elaborate breeze block mooring spaces. Eventually, the housing gives way to some typical Surrey heathland with birch, pines and gorse. The canal follows the contours to reach a new, ornamental office building at Britannia Wharf. If you go under the road bridge you will reach the remains of a small wharf crane, almost the last remnant of the wood trade that continued into the 1940s. The canal now enters a straight section to the skewed Chertsey Road Bridge. The area to the left here was the site of Spanton's Wood Yard, one of the major and last users of the canal. Beyond is Boundary Road, formerly the home of the Woking Gasworks, the single biggest customer of the canal in the twentieth century. At one stage the trade was so brisk (at about 14,000 tons p.a.) that a tramway was built to carry coal from the canal to the works and, presumably, ashes and tar back to the canal. The works were opened in 1892 and closed in 1936. The original Chertsey Road Bridge was built in 1792 but by the turn of this century this and a number of the others around Woking were falling down, a situation that led to some friction between the council and the canal company. The original bridge was replaced by a temporary wooden structure in 1910 while the situation resolved itself. It didn't and the council resorted to an Act to enable it to build new bridges and then charge the company. So in 1922 the present bridge was built. However, as the canal company never had any money, the council was never paid.

Go under the bridge and continue on to the next which carries the Chobham Road. This was also rebuilt in the 1920s at the expense of the council as the original Wheatsheaf Bridge was both falling down and very narrow. To the left are the office blocks, multistorey car parks and shops of Woking. It's said that when the railway opened in 1838, Woking comprised a few houses, a pub and bare heath! If completing your walk here, turn left and follow the signs for the BR station. If continuing to Brookwood, cross both the road and the canal to continue the walk on the right-hand, northern bank.

The walk continues with the canal and Woking to the left. Within 100 yd, the path passes a large car park and goes under a skew bridge. For some distance the canal is bordered by a noisy road. This eventually recedes and the line passes under a small footbridge, Arthur's Bridge. If thirsty, cross the canal for the Bridge Barn pub and restaurant, a converted sixteenth-century barn. Otherwise continue on this side of the canal to pass the front doors of a row of houseboats. After a road bridge, the towpath continues to a brick-built farm accommodation bridge typical of the original style. This is now used solely as a footbridge. The area to the north is Horsell. The canal along here collapsed when a new sewer system was installed in September 1899 and the navigation was closed for six months at a critical time for the survival of the line as a commercial concern beyond Woking. In fact, it never really recovered.

After a set of locks (7–11) collectively known as the Goldsworth Locks, you reach St Johns, formerly the site of the kilns that were used to produce bricks needed at this end of the canal. Here you cross the road and the canal to continue on the left-hand bank. After an iron footbridge, the high-walled railway embankment dominates to the left. The canal swings away from the railway after a couple of hundred yards and broadens to Hermitage Road Bridge. Go through the narrow tunnel under the bridge to a lagoon, home, when I passed, to a group of houseboats. The route now enters countryside with woods on the left and fields to the right. Go under the next bridge (which carries the A322 Bracknell–Guildford road) and up the steps. Cross the canal and turn left to continue the walk along the northern bank. This is Brookwood.

At Brookwood is a 400 acre cemetery, the largest in western Europe. It was built in the 1840s when London's cemeteries were literally overflowing with cholera victims. The London Necropolis & National Mausoleum Company chose the wilds of Woking as the site and on the government's nod bought 2,300 acres of Surrey commonland, most of which was promptly sold off at a vast profit. Bodies and mourners were shipped in from London in huge numbers by the recently built railway line. If you wish to see this particular example of Victorian splendour, turn left at the bridge, go under the railway and the entrance is on the right. However, a good view can be had from the train on the return from Ash Vale.

Brookwood Locks 12–14 now follow in quick succession and within a short distance is an iron road bridge (Sheets Heath Bridge). If finishing the walk at Brookwood you should cross the bridge and go along the road to Brookwood station for trains back to West Byfleet. You are now about 5^1/$_2$ miles from Ash Vale station.

If continuing the walk, go under the bridge. At the next bridge (Pirbright Bridge), cross the road and the canal to continue on the left-hand bank past a house and lock 15. This is the first of the Deepcut Locks, a flight of fourteen over 2 miles which raises the canal 100 ft onto the Surrey Heath. Daniel Defoe visited here in the eighteenth century (before the canal) and described it as 'not good for little but good for nothing'. Defoe may have been aware that the heath was alive with highwaymen. The most famous of all, Dick Turpin, had a hide-out near here from where he made forays on the London to Winchester and Portsmouth roads. Interestingly, I've not seen any references to highwaymen attacking canal boats; maybe the bargees were simply too tough a target?

The canal is now in a deep, quiet slumber. In winter there's a sombre feel to the place. The railway embankment is high to the left and there are extensive woodlands to the right. The canal follows a dank and echoing chasm. Curiously, the railway's amendment Act of 1837 compelled the railway company to build these high banks and walls so that the trains didn't frighten the barge horses. After lock 16, go under Cowshott Bridge to reach locks 17–19. On the other side of the fence to the right is Pirbright Camp, just one part of the extensive area of army encampment in this part of Surrey. The army settled here in 1855 when the first camp was built on the banks of the canal at the Farnborough Road Bridge.

Our way winds through dense woodland to pass locks 20–25. An army swimming pool was built into the canal between locks 22 and 23 and the

A train for Southampton goes under the Frimley Aqueduct

brick walls can still be seen. In 1957 some troops returning from an exercise decided to blow up lock 22, an action which lead to the draining of the pound and deterioration of this part of the canal generally. After a new bridge the canal opens out to form a lagoon with an island (Fred's Ait). Locks 26–28 follow in quick succession, after which is a bungalow formerly a carpenter's shop and forge, and a dry dock rebuilt by Youth Training Scheme workers in 1984. Deepcut Bridge was being renovated as I passed. It was pristine white and very clean. After a cottage to the left, the bank on the right is covered in rhododendrons. It then breaks to an entrance to Wharfenden Lake with its extensive leisure developments. The canal then bends left to pass over Frimley Aqueduct. There are now just 2 miles to Ash Vale.

The aqueduct was built by the London & South Western Railway in 1839 and is 139 ft long. To build it the railway company made a huge cutting up to each side of the canal, then bored through and lined the channels; a process more like tunnelling than aqueduct building. To ensure that the structure was watertight, the canal bed was bricked and a clay 'puddling' layed in the classical fashion. The railway company widened the structure in 1900 and two more arches were added. But by 1925 a sag had developed and a leak started that got progressively worse. A 190 ft long wooden aqueduct was put into place while the main canal was repaired so that the, albeit infrequent, canal traffic could continue. The aqueduct meanwhile was dug out, rebricked, puddled, lined with lead sheets with soldered joints, puddled again and then further layered with bricks. Even this apparent solidity didn't last and the aqueduct had to be relined again during the 1980s. It is worth noting the two stop gates at either end of the aqueduct which can be closed in the event of any further leakage! At the end of the aqueduct, take the metalled lane that bears away from the canal and up to the road. Turn right to cross the bridge. To continue the walk, the path down to the right-hand side of the canal can be found about 10 yd along the road on the left. The King's Head is 50 yd along the road to right.

The canal now takes a straight course with Frimley Lodge Park on the right. In the field can be found the plaque unveiled by the Duke of Kent in May 1991 when he declared the canal officially re-opened. A little way further down the canal, there is an information notice and map of the navigation. Continue along the popular path, passing a small pond, Potter's Pool, to the left. Eventually a railway line (the Staines–Aldershot line) joins the canal, with a housing estate (Mytchett) just beyond. Go under a bridge and along to a point where the canal widens to form Mytchett Lake. The path now goes under a railway bridge. After another couple of hundred yards the railway bends round to pass over the canal again. Just after the bridge, turn right up to a road.

The corrugated-iron shed just after the turn-off point is Ash Vale Barge

The barge *Aldershot* is seen here under construction at A.J. Harmsworth's Ash Vale yard in January 1932

British Waterways

Yard. This was the site of the barge building and repair business run by Alec Harmsworth, who owned the canal for twenty-four years until he died in 1947. Barges were built on this side, while repairs were done on the other. It's said that new boats were produced at about one a year and fell into two types: 'Resos' (residential boats) and 'Oddns' (those without accommodation). They were built of English oak with Columbian pine bottoms to Harmsworth's design. The boats were launched broadside after the remaining struts were knocked out. They were then taken across the canal to be fitted out. The yard was open from 1918 to 1949.

The final stretch is now in view. Bear left and Ash Vale station is about 100 yd downhill on the right. Trains leave for West Byfleet three times an hour even on Sundays. If you want a good view of Brookwood cemetery sit on the right, otherwise the left side offers views of the canal.

Further Explorations

The Surrey and Hampshire county councils must receive the highest praise for their efforts. The whole length of the Basingstoke is good walking and there are a number of specially-built car parks along the way, such as at Odiham (Colt Hill), Crookham Wharf and Wharf Bridge, Aldershot (on the A325). Any of these points can be the start of a quiet and easy walk along the lock-less Hampshire section.

The stretch from Greywell (OS ref: SU 718514) to Odiham is particularly popular. This walk (5 miles) starts at Greywell, a small village $1^1/_4$ miles south-west of junction 5 of the M3. Almost opposite the Fox and Goose pub, a road is signposted to North Warnborough and Odiham. About 20 yd along the road, a sign points left over a stile. This passes over and then down to the canal. Here, to the right, is the entrance to the 1,230 yd Greywell Tunnel. The tunnel was started in 1788 and opened in 1794. At its deepest it is 140 ft below Greywell Hill. It is said to have been rather jerry-built and accusing fingers have been pointed at the local labour employed by John Pinkerton, the contractor. Others say that it suffered from earth movement. Whatever the case, the collapse in 1932 sealed the route to Basingstoke, possibly for ever. It is now a major roosting site for bats. If you peer into the tunnel you can see the barred gate which prevents human access while allowing bats to fly in and out. The portal was given a face-lift in 1976 as part of the European Architectural Heritage Year. A number of springs are tapped along the length of the tunnel and these are the main source of water for the canal. The top pound of the line down to the first lock (Ash Lock in Aldershot) thus acts as a kind of reservoir for the rest of the line.

The eastern portal of Greywell Tunnel

The next 400 yd are a delight. This short stretch fully lives up to the canal's reputation as a nature lover's paradise. In the space of five minutes I saw mallard ducklings, various warblers, numerous dabchicks, swans and a stoat who, no doubt, was viewing the others as potential lunch. After passing the remains of an old lock, at a point where the canal goes through a brick-built channel, the waterway opens out to a winding hole. Within a few yards a small aqueduct carries both canal and towpath over the River Whitewater. This rather insignificant bridge had a minor but important leak for many years before restoration. Shortly after the aqueduct the remains of Odiham Castle are on the left. The castle, popularly known as King John's Castle, was built of stone and flint in the early thirteenth century as a hunting lodge. It was from here that King John rode to Runnymede in June

1215 to sign the Magna Carta. It has been derelict since the fifteenth century.

Back on the canal, the towpath gently winds round the contours to reach North Warnborough Lift Bridge. On some maps this is still labelled as a swing bridge, though there hasn't been one here since 1954. From here, the path again twists to go under the brick-built Swan Bridge. You now pass into more open countryside with only Odiham bypass, away to the left, to remind you that you're still in the twentieth century. Here the canal straightens to pass Lodge Copse Bridge, a simple accommodation bridge, and goes on through pasture to pass underneath Colt Hill Bridge to Odiham Wharf. At weekends you can buy a cup of tea at a kiosk. Alternatively, on the other side of the bridge, the Water Witch pub serves bar meals and has a canalside garden. On summer weekends the society's boat, *John Pinkerton*, provides short trips from the wharf. This fifty-seater boat is operated by enthusiasts and has provided over £100,000 towards the restoration work.

To return to Greywell, you can either retrace your steps or continue past the Water Witch and into the small town of Odiham with its Georgian main street. A footpath sign alongside the George Hotel takes you through some new buildings. Bear left along a narrow path next to a wall and into a field. Turn left and follow a wall and then a hedge to reach a pond. Cross the stile and walk on to reach a road. A footpath sign points you between houses and back to the canal. Turn left, cross the Swan Bridge and then retrace your steps to Greywell.

Further Information

The canal has a very active society which is worthy of attention:

The Surrey & Hampshire Canal Society,
The Spinney,
Meadow Road,
Ashtead,
Surrey KT21 1QR.
Tel: 03722-72631.

It publishes a number of small booklets about the canal, its history and its restoration:

Cansdale, R. & Jebens, D., *A Guide to the Basingstoke Canal.* 1989.

Crocker, G., *A History of the Basingstoke Canal.* 1977.

Gerry, D., *Towpath Walks by the Basingstoke Canal.* 1987.

There is also a useful map of the canal which can be obtained in local shops or from GEOProjects (UK) Ltd, Henley-on-Thames.

2
THE BRECON & ABERGAVENNY CANAL
Talybont to Brecon

Introduction

To build a canal through the Brecon Beacons was pure genius. Whatever it was for; however it was built; whether or not it was a financial success; all irrelevant. Whoever did it was my kind of canal builder. It's simply terrific.

The Brecon & Abergavenny Canal has lived under a number of different names and guises over the years. Correctly speaking, the B&A is merely a section of the Monmouthshire & Brecon. This latter designation (and

The railway viaduct at Crumlin on the Monmouthshire Canal was built in 1857 by Liddle & Gordon to carry the Newport, Abergavenny & Hereford Railway over Ebbw Vale. It crossed the upper reaches of the Crumlin branch. At the time it was the largest viaduct in the world – 1650 ft long and 210 ft high. It was dismantled in 1965

The Boat Museum Archive

British Waterways calls it the M&B) includes the Monmouthshire Canal, a no-longer navigable route which runs from Newport via Cwmbran to Pontymoile, and a branch called the Crumlin Arm, which leaves the main canal at Malpas to head west and then north to Newbridge and Crumlin. The 33 mile long B&A starts at Pontymoile (just south-east of Pontypool) and runs north to Llanfoist near Abergavenny. The line then turns north-west through Gilwern, Llangattock, Llangynidr and Talybont-on-Usk, and on to Brecon.

Here is an easy walk with plenty of good pubs and picnic spots, and so many great views that it could take you all day.

History

It was in 1791 that the industrialists and colliery owners of Monmouthshire saw the advantage of building a canal from Pontnewynydd, just north of Pontypool, to the mouth of the River Usk at the then small port of Newport. After the passage of an Act in June 1792, the Monmouthshire Canal was built to serve the ironworks, limestone quarries and collieries of the area of Pontnewynydd and of Crumlin, to which a branch line had been built. The main canal was 11 miles long and rose 435 ft by forty-one locks.

With the construction work on the Monmouthshire under way, the people to the north started to consider the potential for a canal of their own. One plan that circulated in August 1792 proposed a line from the River Usk at Newbridge to Abergavenny and on to Llanelly near Gilwern. However, it wasn't too long before it was realized that there were advantages in moving the southern end further east to join the Monmouthshire at Pontymoile, just south of Pontypool. The Monmouthshire's proprietors were so convinced of the advantages that they offered the new canal's promoters a £3,000 inducement to continue. They also promised to supply the water to the lower pound that would run from Pontymoile to Llangynidr. All these matters were discussed and agreed at a meeting held on 15 October 1792, by which time it was also agreed to extend the waterway further north to Brecon.

The proposed line, of what at the time was known as the Abergavenny Canal, was surveyed by Thomas Dadford, Junior, son of the Thomas Dadford who had built the Glamorganshire Canal. At the time, Dadford was employed as engineer to the Monmouthshire Company and it was it which paid him for undertaking the survey. His recommended line was 33 miles in length, from Brecon to a junction with the Monmouthshire at Pontymoile. The plan included three tramroads: Gilwern to Beaufort;

Gilwern to Glangrwyne; and Llanfoist Wharf to Abergavenny Bridge.

Dadford's survey was approved at a meeting in November 1792 and the Act received Royal Assent in March 1793. The authorized capital for the Brecknockshire & Abergavenny Canal was £100,000, with approval to raise a further £50,000 if it was needed. The Act included powers to build tramroads up to a distance of 8 miles from the canal. While the Monmouthshire attracted shareholders from a wide area, the B&A was a much more parochial affair, with most of its support coming from local sources. There were some shareholders, however, such as the Duke of Beaufort and Sir Charles Morgan, who held shares in the Monmouthshire Canal, and the members of the Wilkins family of the The Old Bank, Brecon, had interests in a number of other Welsh canals. Right from the beginning, the B&A was different from the majority of the other canals in south Wales in that it was not intended as an industrial line. Whereas most of the recently constructed waterways were built to carry iron and coal out to seaports, the B&A was primarily built to carry coal, lime, manure and agricultural produce inland to Brecon and other places along the canal.

Construction work started in 1794 when a tramroad from the coal mines at Gelli Felen in the Clydach valley to Glangrwyne was built by John Dadford, Thomas junior's brother. Strangely, and much to the annoyance of the Monmouthshire which had handed over its £3,000 in March 1794, the building work on the canal itself wasn't started until early 1797. Dadford junior was appointed engineer, a post he took up full-time when the Monmouthshire was completed at the end of 1798. The first stretch to be built was the embankment and aqueduct over the River Clydach at Gilwern. The length between Gilwern and Llangynidr was opened in November 1797.

Additional funds were raised in April 1799 by making extra calls on the existing shares and this enabled the completion of the section between Gilwern and Brecon. The main water supply for the line was then available from the River Usk via a weir just above Brecon. Alan Stevens notes that the water from the weir goes through a culvert that passes right under the town to the head of the canal.

By the time Brecon was reached in December 1800, the company was once again running short of funds. The cost so far was £120,000, including the tramroads. But some income was forthcoming from the shipment of coal to Brecon along the opened route and the company paid a dividend of £1 17s. 6d. in 1802. However, more cash was needed if the line was to be extended to Pontymoile. A further Act was obtained in 1804 providing powers to raise another £80,000 and by the beginning of 1805 the canal, now with Thomas Cartwright as engineer, was extended to Govilon Wharf.

Once again construction work stopped through lack of cash. It was estimated that £50,000 was needed to complete the line and it wasn't until

This peaceful scene at Gilwern, thought to have been taken in the early 1900s, perhaps suggests that the once busy wharf had already declined

The Boat Museum Archive

1809 that this was forthcoming, mostly from one individual, Richard Crawshay, who granted a loan of £30,000. With this the third engineer on the project, William Crossley, resurveyed the line from Govilon to Pontymoile. The work started at Pontymoile in about 1810 working north and was completed on 7 February 1812. At the official opening, the company committee boarded a boat and passed from the Monmouthshire to the B&A amid 'the aclamation [sic] of a very numerous body of the inhabitants'. The total cost of the canal was about £200,000.

There were problems with scouring of the foundations of the aqueduct at Pontymoile and it had to be demolished and rebuilt before the canal was completely opened, but by 1813 the line was fully operational. Toll receipts were now totalling nearly £9,000 p.a. and trade was increasing, albeit rather slowly. Although dividends had reached £3 per share in 1808–09, none were paid between 1811 and 1817. This was done to allow the company to clear its debts. Even at this stage concerns were being expressed over low profitability, and as part of an ambitious programme to encourage traffic, a whole succession of tramroads were built to link with the canal. In other schemes to stimulate business, agreements were forged with ironworks to carry ore free if finished goods was then carried on the canal, drawbacks were given to encourage long-distance traffic, and other deals were made in which tolls were reduced in exchange for guaranteed trade. All this had the effect of increasing revenue to £11,021 in 1818–19 and enabling the company to pay a £2 dividend. But by the early 1820s trade was again becoming hard to find, so that even though the company was able to pay a £4 dividend in 1821–2, by 1823 revenue was down to £10,221. In that year the company carried 86,944 tons of cargo on the canal and 27,024 tons on the tramroads. Most of this traffic was coal, coke and iron, with lesser amounts of lime and limestone. The later 1820s saw a marginal improvement in the situation, with the dividend peaking at £9 per £150 share in 1825–6, albeit at the cost of cutting staff wages. But these were the peak years and from then on trade declined, a situation not helped by more aggressive competition for the Nantyglo iron trade from the Monmouthshire.

By 1833 trade was definitely on the decline and dividends were down to £4 per share. The B&A shareholders resolved to amalgamate with the Monmouthshire Company, a situation helped by the fact that the influential ironworks owner Joseph Bailey was on the board of both. Despite the continuing threat of unnecessary competition and the fact that the companies' representatives had established the basis of a deal, the B&A shareholders could not agree to the terms offered, in which the Monmouthshire was to guarantee dividends. Thus the proposed merger was dropped. There was, however, a better understanding between the two companies and both prospered for a brief period after the talks. During most of the 1830s the B&A was able to pay an annual dividend of £5 to £5 10s.

By the 1840s the influence of the newly-built railways was beginning to be felt. At one stage the committee considered selling the line to the Welsh Midland Railway. However, the WMR was dissolved without the deal going through. Instead, a survey was made to assess the potential for putting a railway line along the canal bank between Brecon and Pontypool. This also came to nothing. Various other plans and potential sales followed in the course of the 1850s, during which the section of the Monmouthshire Canal from Pontymoile to Pontnewynydd was closed and that company changed its name to the Monmouthshire Railway & Canal Company (MR&CCo). Many of the tramroads built by the Monmouthshire were converted into railways. Other railways such as the Brecon & Merthyr and the Newport, Abergavenny & Hereford were also built, taking much of the traffic from the canals. Dividends for B&A shareholders fell from £6 per share in 1855–6 to 10s. per share in 1861–2. A further reason for the steady decline in traffic along the line was the closure of many of the old ironworks connected to the canals.

The B&A responded in the only way open to it, and that was to reduce tolls. On 1 February 1863 the rates for coal were reduced from 2d. per ton per mile to just 1/2d. But with things not improving, the committee offered to sell the canal to the Monmouthshire Company for £61,200. This deal was finalized on 29 September 1865. Although there were advantages for the two lines joining forces against the competition, the Monmouthshire was also keen to gain access to the water that flowed from the River Usk into the B&A. The Monmouthshire not only needed this supply to keep its remaining line open but found an additional income in selling supplies to industry along the canal.

The independence of the new company did not last long. In 1880 the Monmouthshire (and hence the B&A) was taken over by the Great Western Railway Company, which was plainly more interested in railways than canals. By the turn of the twentieth century traffic was reduced to about a boat a week. The last commercial traffic to pay a toll on the B&A at Llangynidr was in 1933.

The Monmouthshire and Brecon Canal was taken over by the British Transport Commission in 1948 and, like many other canals, rescue was slow in coming. The BTC Act of 1949 closed the Crumlin branch of the Monmouthshire Canal and most of this is now derelict. A further Act of 1954 closed another portion near Cwmbran. In the Report of the Board of Survey for the Commission published in 1955, the two lines, under the title of the Monmouthshire & Brecon, were officially classified as 'Remainder'. This led to the abandonment of the line in 1962. However, this action drew the attention of some local enthusiasts to the potential of the waterway. After being taken over by British Waterways (BW) in 1963, restoration work was started. The 1968 Transport Act still considered the B&A as a 'remainder' canal and as such the line has no legal protection. Despite this, the line has gradually been restored to health. In 1969 there was agreement between the Monmouthshire and Breconshire county councils and BW on the restoration of the canal as an amenity. In 1970 a low bridge at Talybont was replaced by a steel drawbridge and the lock at Brynich was rebuilt and fitted with hydraulic paddle gear. Now the whole line from Pontymoile to Brecon is open for navigation and is a highly popular route through the very beautiful Brecon Beacons National Park.

The Walk

Start:	Talybont-on-Usk (OS ref: SO 113227)
Finish:	Brecon (OS ref: SO 045285)
Distance:	7 miles/11 1/4 km
Map:	OS Outdoor Leisure Map 11 (Brecon Beacons National Park Central Area)

Outward: Brecon to Talybont-on-Usk via Red & White Buses no. 21 (enquiries: 0633-265100)
Car park: Brecon: large and well-signposted
Public transport: BR goes to Abergavenny and from there the Red & White Buses no. 21 goes to both Brecon and Talybont.

I joined the canal at the Traveller's Rest pub on the B4558, south of the village of Talybont towards Cwm Crawnon. A quick ascent of the steps from the beer garden brings you to the canal. Before starting the walk enthusiastic towpathers may wish to turn left along the left-hand bank, for about 1/3 mile to see the Ashford Tunnel. This, the only one on the B&A, is 375 yd long and is masonry lined. Boats were 'legged' through while the horses took the road that runs alongside. I'm told that halfway through the roof of the tunnel dips precariously and passing boaters have to duck rather rapidly or receive a hefty clout about the head. To start the walk proper, return to the Traveller's Rest and walk along the right-hand bank. Within a short distance you go under a road bridge (no. 142). This was formerly a stone arch bridge but it collapsed and has been replaced by this steel girder bridge.

Almost immediately the canal reaches Talybont Wharf (on the opposite bank). This was once a busy spot! What appears to be a road just above the wharf is in fact the end of the former Bryn Oer tramroad. The wharf was used to tranship both limestone from the Trevil limestone quarry and coal from the Bryn Oer colliery near Rhymney, some 12 miles distant. The coal was taken north along the canal to Brecon and, via the Hay tramway, to

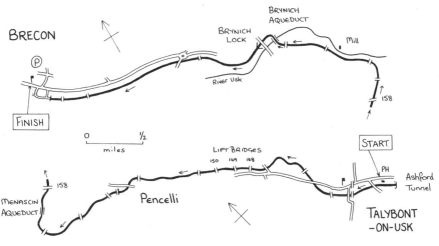

The Brecon & Abergavenny Canal

Kington and Hay. The limestone, meanwhile, was burnt in the limekilns which were positioned just beyond the tramway. The tramroad, which first opened in 1815, can be followed from bridge 143 up to the Talybont reservoir, a walk that is described in John Norris' canal guide (see below). After passing a pipe bridge, which carries water from Talybont reservoir to Newport, go under the former Brecon & Merthyr Railway. The White Hart pub is to the right. Bridge 143 (White Hart Bridge) follows shortly thereafter, its sagging arch now neatly supported by a series of wrought-iron rails. It is this bridge that should be crossed to follow the Bryn Oer tramroad. Those on their way to Brecon, however, should continue by following the canal sharp right and over a narrow aqueduct which crosses Afon (i.e. River) Caerfanell. The Star Inn on the right is recommended by CAMRA.

Talybont Lift Bridge (no. 144) is comparatively recent. Originally on this site was a wooden lift bridge. However, during the period when the canal was unnavigable, it was replaced by a fixed bridge which had clearance of just 2 ft. The present bridge is the second to be built here since 1970. The bridge is electrically operated. A motor winds a wire rope onto a drum to raise the deck. Mischievous souls will note that it only functions with the aid of a British Waterways key.

The route continues under Benaiah Bridge and then Chilson Bridge. This has a neat pile of stop planks positioned underneath. Along this stretch there are some simply wonderful curves and bends, as if the canal really wants to be a meandering river when it grows up. The whole ambience of peace and solitude is ably supported by the lush green Usk Valley to the right. To maintain a level course through such undulating country was a splendid feat but it was achieved at the expense of this winding route, beautiful for us but probably quite tiresome for a boatman with cargo to deliver. After bridge 147 (Cross Oak Bridge) you come to the first manually-operated drawbridge. Bridges 148–50 (Cross Oak, Gethinog and Penawr lift bridges) are all drawbridges of a similar style. These aren't the originals but were built to Dadford's design. The bridges are counterbalanced by means of weights on the end, mounted between the two upper beams, and are operated by a chain fixed to the end of one of the beams. This chain is worked by the lockgear-like system that can be seen at leg-level on one side.

After the third lift bridge, the remains of a drain plug and windlass can be seen on the near right. To the uninitiated this looks like two bits of old railway line stuck into the ground. There are several more between here and Brecon and only one, near the Brynich Aqueduct, still has most of its mechanism in place. The canal now goes under a stone bridge (Penawr Bridge) and on to a stop point, where the narrowness of the channel allows stop planks to be used to isolate sections of the waterway. Bridge 152 (Castle Bridge) is typical of all the fine B&A accommodation bridges; simple but with great character. Of interest here are the still extant metal

The Brynich Aqueduct carries the canal over the River Usk just south of Brecon

notices, erected by the Great Western Railway to warn potential users that the bridge has insufficient strength to carry a 'heavy motor car'.

The outskirts of Pencelli are announced by a large building to the left which sits near the remains of Pencelli Castle. This was formerly the seat of a medieval lord. Bridge 153 (Cross Keys Bridge) is newer than 152, can definitely take the weight of heavy motor cars and is none the better for it. Pass the canalside beer garden of the Royal Oak and go under Pencelli Bridge to reach a winding hole, a slipway and Pencelli Wharf. Just beyond the slipway is the final drawbridge (no. 155). Now go under two more bridges (Low Bridge and Llan-brynean Bridge) to reach Menascin Aqueduct. This entire stretch was extensively renovated during the winter of 1992, with the channel of the canal being relined to stop seepage. The towpath has also been upgraded. The modern method for laying canal channels in areas where leakage may occur is to lay a bed of concrete which is sealed with a plastic membrane and then protected by a thin layer of concrete on top.

Storehouse Bridge (no. 158) is a rather utilitarian structure dating from 1958 but it gives you your first view (left) of the Brecon Beacons and the start of some of the most scenic waterway in the country. Immediately beyond bridge 159 is the Cambrian Cruisers marina at Ty Newydd. The canal then swings left under bridge 160 and on to offer superb views to the right, firstly of Llanhamlach church and then of the River Usk which is now literally a stone's throw away. At one point the river passes over a weir to produce a series of white-water rapids. Bridge 161 (Bell Ear Bridge) has a sagging arch, thought to be due to subsidence of the abutments, and is neatly braced in the same way as White Hart Bridge was earlier.

Cross the canal at the next bridge (Turn Bridge: no. 162) to continue along the left-hand bank and on to Brynich Aqueduct. Just before it there is an overflow weir and, for those who have been looking out for one, an almost intact windlass. The aqueduct itself is a fine four-arch structure which was opened in 1800. Originally the channel had a masonry lining and was puddled with clay in the standard way. Only with renovations in the 1970s was the channel lined with concrete which can be seen clearly stretching out from the canal banks. The massiveness of the aqueduct and its superb position over the broad River Usk can only impress. It does, however, appear to be rather old-fashioned in style. It is, Alan Stevens points out, much more like James Brindley's Sow Aqueduct on the Staffordshire & Worcestershire than Thomas Telford's Pont Cysyllte on the Llangollen, even though it is contemporary with the latter. From the aqueduct there are good views of the river, and of the Brynich (road) Bridge to the left. It is possible to clamber down from the right side of the canal to the river's edge to see the aqueduct itself and, through its arches, Brynich Bridge.

After the aqueduct the canal makes a rather abrupt left turn and moves on to Cefn Brynich Bridge and Brynich Lock, which ends the $7\frac{1}{2}$ mile long pound that has stretched all the way from Llangynidr. Like the other locks on the B&A, Brynich is about $9\frac{1}{2}$ ft wide and 65 ft long. It has a rise/fall of 10 ft and some of the prettiest winding gear of any lock anywhere. After passing a small picnic area, the canal moves on with some magnificent views of the Brecon Beacons to the left. The highest peak in the range is the rather flat-topped mountain to the right of the others. This is Pen-y-fan and is 2,906 ft above sea level. From here on the towpath will be plagued by road noise as the canal bends right to meet the A40. Go under Brynich Bridge (no. 164) and then the bypass bridge which is so long that it could almost be classified as a tunnel. It is now a mile to the next bridge and 300 yd before you reach it is a long row of limekilns in the bank behind the towpath. These are invisible from the canal but if you walk on to reach a driveway you can turn left to walk back to see them. Meanwhile, to go on to Brecon continue along the canal past the rugby pitches and on to Watton Bridge (no. 165). This has a curious extra arch on the right-hand side which was built to accommodate the Hay tramway which followed the course of the canal into Brecon. On the other side of the bridge is the former Watton Wharf, now the site of some industrial premises.

Enter Brecon by walking past some terraced houses and going under the final bridge: no. 166, Gasworks Bridge. There is now just a short stretch of canal remaining and this has been used as a temporary mooring site. It is also home to Dragonfly Cruises. The canal comes to an end a little further on. Here a culverted feeder arrives from the River Usk, having been piped under the streets of Brecon from a weir half a mile upriver. The canal originally continued along the line of the road ahead for about 200 yd, ending in a side basin to the right. You should also go that way. Turn right at the end and follow Danygear Road round to pass a four-storey warehouse, dated 1892, which is one of the few surviving canal wharf buildings. At the end of the road, turn left to reach the High Street.

Further Explorations

The entire 33^1/$_2$ miles of the B&A is open for walking. Those lucky enough to hit a sunny weekend could well manage the entire length from Pontymoile to Brecon in two days, assuming that transport at both ends can be arranged. A halfway point would be somewhere between Abergavenny and Crickhowell. There are good bus connections all the way along and British Rail operates between Abergavenny and Pontypool, and on to Newport.

For those with less time there is a fine walk of just over 9 miles between Llangattock and Llanfoist which makes the most of the Red & White Buses bus no. 21, this time between Abergavenny and Crickhowell (enquiries: 0633-265100). The whole walk can be found on OS Outdoor Leisure Map 13: Brecon Beacons Eastern Area.

From the Crickhowell bus-stop walk past the Beaufort Arms and turn left. Continue past the pink-washed Dragon Hotel then turn right along Bridge Street. This passes the Bridge End Inn. Go across the River Usk via the fine bridge. At the far end go straight ahead and follow a signposted footpath into a field. This comes out past the Church of St Catwg to a road. Bear right and take the road which is signposted to Ffawyddog. Go uphill to reach the canal at Ffawyddog Bridge (no. 116) and turn left along the left-hand bank. From here there is a fine view back across Crickhowell to the Black Mountains.

The canal soon bends right and then left to go over a small aqueduct which crosses the stream from Nant Onnau. Shortly thereafter is Llangattock Wharf with its substantial limekilns. The wharf was built at the end of a tramroad from limestone quarries above it. The kilns were then supplied with coal from the canal. From here the B&A winds through some fine country and passes a series of bridges (nos 113–105) with great views over the valley to the left. The start of Gilwern (where the construction work on the canal began in 1797) is marked by bridge 104 (Auckland Bridge) and then Gilwern Wharf, home to Castle Narrowboats, on the far bank. At the far end of the Clydach dock is an arch through which the mile-long feeder canal arrives from the River Clydach. The dock here was an important canal/railway interchange basin and was served by a branch of the Glyngywyney to Brynmawr tramway. Coal from Gelli-felen, pig iron from Ebbw Vale and limestone from Black Rock in the Clydach Gorge were all transhipped here. Just beyond the basin, the line continues over Clydach Gorge on Thomas Dadford's massive embankment. The River Clydach goes underneath through a 100 yd long tunnel. The embankment also goes over the route of the old tramroad. If you take some steps to the left just after the basin, you can descend to see the tunnel. In fact you can go further still and John Norris (see below) describes a walk which starts at the tunnel. On the south (far) side of the embankment was the Clydach Iron Company's wharf, where the tramroad ran from the Llanmarch collieries.

At the end of the embankment the canal bends left and crosses a spill weir with a magnificent tumbling waterfall shoot which carries water down to the Clydach below. The next bridge, Gilwern Bridge, is actually more of a tunnel and towpathers are forced to walk up to and then across the road. The canal now leaves Gilwern and goes under the Heads of the Valleys Road (A465). This whole section between Gilwern and Govilon has seen some extensive renovation during the winter of 1992, with a concrete channel being laid. At Govilon the canal passes over two small aqueducts in quick succession. The first goes over a minor road and the second over the stream that comes down Cwm Llanwenarth. The towpath changes sides at Govilon Bridge and goes on to pass under the old skewed railway bridge, which once carried the Heads of the Valleys line, to reach Govilon Wharf. From 1805 to 1812, when the canal company was desperately short of cash, Govilon was the terminus of the line. It was also the terminus of the Llanvihangel tramroad which connected the canal with Hereford. This was built in 1819 to carry coal. The wharf was supplied by Bailey's tramroad which delivered coal and iron ore from Nantyglo and Brynmawr. All that remains of this feverish activity today is an old warehouse building and the boats belonging to members of the Govilon Boat Club.

The towpath changes sides at Govilon Quarry Bridge to return to the left-hand bank and the start of a stunning section of waterway. You're perched high above the valley with the town of Abergavenny now visible through the trees to the left and the tree-covered hillside continuing ever higher to the right. This lofty position is not without problems for the long-suffering British Waterways. The frequency of the stop gates and stop plank grooves along this stretch only suggests the problems. This whole length is very prone to breaches. The section just beyond the White House Turn (where

The formerly busy Llanfoist Wharf, near Abergavenny, is now a tranquil rural retreat

the canal appears to head straight into the hill, only to suddenly turn left) was breached in 1975. It took many of the downhill trees with it and blocked the line for some time. Following that breach the canal was lined with concrete, a move which will hopefully prevent such incidents in the future.

It is now just a short stroll to Llanfoist Wharf, one of the canal system's photographic hot spots. The warehouse and wharf-manager's house are still standing in this delightful place. Llanfoist was once the terminal for Hill's tramroad which brought iron ore up from Newport to Hill's Ironworks at Blaenavon and carried finished iron products back down. The tramroad contained no fewer than four inclined planes. The wood-decked bridge to the left is Tod's Bridge (no. 95). The tramroad crossed the canal via the bridge and passed down a further incline to join the Llanvihangel tramroad near Llanfoist village.

To return to Abergavenny don't go under Tod's Bridge but take the steps left which descend to Llanfoist village. At the road turn right and follow it around under the Merthyr road and over the Usk Bridge into Abergavenny.

Further Information

The Brecon & Abergavenny is a justifiably popular canal that is ably served by its own supporters trust:

The Monmouthshire, Brecon & Abergavenny Canals Trust,

6 Glamorgan Close,

Llantwit Major,

South Glamorgan CF6 9GG.

The trust produces a newsletter which updates members on canal matters, including the progress of the planned restoration of the line to Newport.

Two books which describe the delights of the B&A are:

Norris, John, *The Brecon & Abergavenny Canal.* J.R. Norris, The Birches off Wickham Hill, Hurstpierpoint, West Sussex BN6 9NP, 1991.

Stevens, R.A., *Brecknock & Abergavenny and Monmouthshire Canals. Towpath Guide No. 2.* Goose & Son, Cambridge, 1974.

There is also the more learned:

Gladwin, D.D. & J.M., *Canals of the Welsh Valleys and their Tramroads.* Oakwood Press, 1990.

3
THE BRIDGWATER & TAUNTON CANAL
Taunton to Bridgwater

Introduction

The short length of canal that connects the two West Country towns of Taunton and Bridgwater was originally built as just one part of an altogether grander scheme. In 1810 the Grand Western Canal was being built to join Exeter with Taunton, and the Kennet & Avon was being finished to give a continuous waterway between London and Bristol. The promoters of the Bristol & Taunton Canal saw the potential for a fully navigable route all the way from London to Exeter. Sadly this was a vision that with the dawning of an altogether different view on the wisdom of canal investment was never to materialize.

At its southern end, the B&T starts at Firepool Lock, not far from Taunton railway station. Here there is access to the River Tone and formerly a junction with the Grand Western Canal. The line starts by heading east under the M5 to Creech St Michael. Gradually the canal bends north through North Newton and Fordgate before winding around Huntworth and the westerly edge of Bridgwater to Bridgwater Docks. Beyond the docks, boats were able to enter the River Parrett and hence travel on to the Bristol Channel.

The countryside is flat and gentle between the two towns and this is a flat and gentle stroll. Keep it for a warm summer day and take a picnic.

History

In the days of canal mania, the people of the south-west seemed almost desperate to build a canal and schemes abounded. There were two prominent projects. The first aimed to connect the north and south coasts of the Devon/Cornwall peninsula in order to avoid the hazards of Land's End. The second proposed a continuous waterway between London and Exeter. As part of this latter scheme, at least two proposals were made to link Taunton with Bristol or the Bristol Channel. The first, the Bristol & Western Canal, was proposed in December 1792. The route was to be from the River Avon at Morgan's Pill, near Bristol, to Taunton. The rival Taunton & Uphill Canal would exit to the Bristol Channel at Uphill near Weston-super-Mare. In both cases, the opportunity was seen for a direct navigation between Bristol and Exeter, continuing from Taunton to the River Exe via the Grand Western Canal. Both groups surveyed their routes and both were defeated by vigorous opposition from landowners who feared that the schemes would affect land drainage or irrigation or both.

By 1810 the situation had changed. The K&A, which joined London and Bristol via the Thames and Avon, was now open and the GWC was finally under construction. The prospects for a continuous waterway between London and Exeter again looked good. John Rennie, who had been involved with both the K&A and the GWC, reviewed the proposed Bristol & Western Union Canal, later to be called the Bristol & Taunton Canal. 'No line of country', he claimed, 'can be more favourable for a navigable canal.' He proposed a level ship canal from a lock on the Avon at Morgan's Pill to run north of Nailsea through a 600 yd tunnel at Clevedon and one of 1,050 yd at Bandwell, to reach the south side of the River Parrett at Bridgwater. There a short branch would link canal and river. The line would then ascend two locks to cross the Parrett near Huntworth and run via Creech St Michael to join the GWC at Taunton.

As usual there were objections. A meeting of landowners in January 1811 concluded that it would harm their interests and hazard drainage. There were also objections from the conservators of the River Tone. The Tone navigation joined the River Parrett at Burrow Bridge to form a continuous waterway between Taunton and Bridgwater and thus to the Bristol Channel. This route was originally made navigable in 1717. The Tone had a some-what tarnished image as the navigation was in debt to its conservators who enjoyed a sizable repayment of interest. Despite this, the line was of great benefit to the people of Taunton who were able to import coal from South Wales and other goods from Bristol at greatly reduced cost. When the new canal was proposed, the conservators saw that their trade would be seriously affected and they decided on opposition.

The Bristol & Taunton Canal Act was passed in 1811. Rennie suggested a total of £410,896 and, in the rush of enthusiasm, the offer was fully sub-scribed. To placate objectors the company was required to not do any work at Clevedon or on the Parrett until it had finished the lengths on either side. On top of this the whole canal had to be completed within four years of the

Act being passed. As for the Tone, the new company had within three months of the Act to acquire the outstanding debt. This it eventually did but by 1822 construction work on the canal had still not started. This meant that the four year proviso had lapsed and with it went the desire to build the entire section from Bridgwater to Bristol.

By March 1822 a shareholder's meeting agreed that as the Tone regularly became unnavigable due to drought in summer or floods in winter, there was still potential for building a canal from Huntworth to Taunton as a useful alternative. Following an injunction against building the canal by some local farmers, the company obtained a second Act of Parliament in 1824. This confirmed the building of the new canal, allowed the company to lock down into the Parrett at Huntworth and to build a basin there. The new company promptly asked the GWC to extend its line to Taunton or allow it to build the intervening section itself. This might then provide the long-desired line from the Bristol Channel to Exeter. So, by 1824, the Bridgwater & Taunton was under construction. For a length of 13^1/$_2$ miles the engineer

The sale of hay could be an important additional source of income for many canals, particularly in the latter days when barge traffic may have declined. The hay collecting here was photographed near Huntworth

Kodak Museum, The Boat Museum Archive

James Hollinworth estimated the cost at £34,135. Locks were built at the slightly odd 54 ft x 13 ft (with a draft of 3 ft) which meant a normal craft load of 22 tons. The line was speedily cut with no significant problems. It was opened on 3 January 1827 when a barge, flags flying, arrived at a chilly Taunton to be welcomed by a cheering crowd. The canal had cost about £97,000 to build, with £57,000 having been raised from shareholders. The remaining funds were borrowed and weren't finally paid off until 1837.

The opening of the canal was not greeted with enthusiasm by the Tone conservators and there now followed a period of unseemly squabbling. The Tone conservators were intent on hindering the canal's water supply and at one point the B&T was reduced to breaking down the river bank at Taunton to forcibly connect the canal with the river. The conservators knew that the B&T was the more direct and least problematical line to Bridgwater and in order to maintain their share of business they reduced their tolls, even though the navigation still had unpaid debt (ironically now owed to the canal company). The B&T objected but lost the battle in court. In response it served notice on 28 August 1827 that it was going to take over the navigation under powers provided in the 1811 Act which were, it contested, renewed in the 1824 Act. It offered the payment required of it by the Act but was rejected. Things then got serious. In November 1827 the canal company forcibly took charge of the river, returned the tolls to their former rate and stopped all routine maintenance. The courts ordered that the B&T's action had been outside the time permitted by the 1811 Act. The conservators repossessed the river in July 1830 and once again reduced the tolls and kept the canal as short of water as they possible could. To cement this action, literally, a dam was built to separate canal and river at Firepool Lock below Taunton bridge. Although forced to take the dam down, the conservators threatened legal action on any boats or vessels entering the Tone from the canal.

The canal company made a final offer of purchase in November 1831. It was again rejected. The matter was then resolved in the House of Commons. An authorizing Act, passed in July 1832, enabled the canal company to purchase the Tone for just £2,000. The B&T also settled all the outstanding small debts, rebuilt two bridges, built a direct canal between the Tone and the Grand Western Canal, carried out various other odd jobs and, of course, cancelled the remaining debt which it now owed to itself. The conservators still retained the right to an annual inspection of the navigation and if it was not 'properly maintained' had the right to repossess the river. The B&T was now left with an open-ended requirement to keep the Tone maintained. At the time the river was carrying 39,516 tons p.a. and collecting tolls of £2,194. About 13,000 tons of this trade, mostly in coal, was unloaded at Ham Mills for towns as far south as Ilminster. However, when the Chard Canal was opened from Creech St Michael to Ilminster in 1841,

Bridgwater Docks, here shown in the early 1900s, were opened following the extension of the canal from its original terminus near Huntworth in 1841. Although largely unused during the course of the twentieth century, the area is now being redeveloped
M. Smith, The National Monuments Record

almost all of this traffic moved to the new route. Given that the B&T was preferred to the Tone for through traffic, almost the only business left on the river was that coming loaded or unloaded on the Parrett navigation.

While the traffic on the Tone was declining, that on the canal was increasing. By 1842 118,216 tons of goods were moved with a toll income of £8,239. But such riches were short-lived. In May 1836 an Act was passed for the Bristol & Exeter Railway, with branches to Dunball Wharf and Bridgwater (a branch to Taunton was approved in 1845). In response, the canal company came out fighting. In 1837 it obtained an Act which allowed it to extend its line from Huntworth to its present junction with the Parrett at Bridgwater. In doing this, the Huntworth lock and basin were closed, an extra mile of canal was built round the town and the ship dock was excavated. The full line as it is today was opened on 25 March 1841 with the peeling of bells, the firing of cannon, the playing of the national anthem, and the consumption of much 'roast beef and plum pudding'.

The new extension was a very risky venture given the likely traffic levels and the potential of the railway. With a cost of £100,000, heavy mortgages were incurred and as the profit in the first year was just £1,396, there was little hope of repayment. The situation was made worse when the railway between Bridgwater and Taunton was opened on 1 July 1842. This forced the B&T to lower its tolls and the company even agreed to pay the GWC a fee to persuade it to use the canal rather than the railway as the source of imported coal. As the railway network, and the facilities it required, expanded, so the future of the canal looked ever more bleak. In 1845 the company concluded that as it couldn't beat them it would join them and proposed the Bridgwater & Taunton Canal Railway, in which the bed of the canal would be converted into a railway track. Various other canal companies joined in; for example, one plan in association with the Kennet & Avon proposed the London, Devizes & Bridgwater Direct Line. The whole scheme was to be called the West of England Central & Channels Junction Railway; able to carry passengers from London to Penzance. None of these schemes came to fruition, however, and the company appointed a receiver.

As a consequence of this action, debts to the GWC as part of the fee deal worked out in 1842, weren't paid and in 1848 the latter started to use the railway instead. This further reduced trade along the B&T. By the 1850s the traffic had switched dramatically to the railways. In 1851 the company listed its debts as £118,130. The company's receiver sought and obtained an agreement with the Bristol & Exeter Railway Company which eventually led to the sale of the B&T in 1866, the railway finally gaining possession on 8 April 1867 for a price of £64,000. This sum paid off the mortgagees and, after the various debts had been sorted out, provided a small amount for the shareholders. The railway company started its period of ownership with a flourish. It built a new landing stage at Bridgwater dock where a steam crane transferred coals to a horse tramway (later converted to a locomotive line) which connected with its own main line. But in 1876 the Bristol & Exeter Railway amalgamated with the Great Western Railway and the canal went into decline. The opening of the Severn railway tunnel in 1886 meant that the sea trade to the Bridgwater dock decreased, as coal now came from South Wales by train. By 1890 the canal tonnage stood at 13,809 (compared with 59,806 in 1852) and was restricted to coal and timber. The final *coup de grâce* occurred between 1896 and 1901 when the canal ran short of water and many loads were forced to go by train. In 1905, when water levels were restored, customers were loath to transfer back. By 1907, tonnage was officially recorded as zero.

Thereafter the canal remained virtually unused. During the Second World War the War Office turned it into a line of defence, building numerous pillboxes and replacing twelve swing bridges with fixed bridges strong enough to bear the weight of army vehicles. The Tone meanwhile remained navigable if unused. Both lines were nationalized in 1948 and allowed to decline further, although the waterway was maintained as a water supply channel for Bridgwater. In the review by the Board of Survey in 1955 both the canal and the Tone were placed into Group 3, 'Waterways having insufficient commercial prospects to justify their retention', a valid comment given the criteria applied. Although the Bowes Committee of 1958 thought that the canal may be suitable for redevelopment, no significant improvements resulted. Similarly, the condition of the canal did not improve with the transfer of ownership to BW in 1963. Although the Transport Act of 1968 still considered the B&T outside of those worthy of maintenance for commercial or cruising purposes, by that time the B&T Canal Restoration Group (later the Somerset Inland Waterways Society) had been formed and gradually attitudes and enthusiasms were changing. Today, BW is working with Somerset County Council, Taunton Deane Borough Council and Sedgemoor District Council to restore the line and to make it into the public amenity that it should be.

The Walk

Start:	Taunton BR station (OS ref: ST 228254)
Finish:	Bridgwater Docks (OS ref: ST 298376)
Distance:	14 1/4 miles/23 km
Maps:	OS Landranger 193 (Taunton & Lyme Regis) and 182 (Weston-super-Mare & Bridgwater)
Return:	BR Bridgwater to Taunton (enquiries: 0934-621131) – trains run on Sundays; or Southern National bus no. 21/21A – runs 1/2 hourly but not on Sundays (enquiries: 0823-272033)
Car park:	Taunton or Bridgwater BR stations
Public transport:	BR serves both towns.

From Taunton station turn left under two rail bridges. After these turn left past the Royal Mail pub. Turn left again along Canal Road with the cattle market to the right. After a further 1/4 mile, the road reaches the canal at Firepool Lock, the site of the junction with the River Tone. Both the river and the lock are to the right of the bridge that crosses the canal at this point. Ahead the B&T canal heads towards Bridgwater. To the left of the bridge the course of the canal appears to make an abrupt turn into Firepool Lock. In fact, when operational this point (the line of a low brick wall) was a stop lock and the junction between the B&T and the Grand Western Canal.

The GWC was one part of the scheme to link the Bristol and English channels. In its original plan it was to run from the B&T to the River Exe. However, the canal faced considerable financial problems so that by 1838 the line that opened ran from Firepool Lock to Tiverton. It never reached either the Exe or the English Channel. The canal as built, however, was an extraordinary venture. It had no fewer than seven vertical lifts and an incline plane. One of those lifts, the Taunton Lift, lay just beyond the junction on the site of one of the railway lines behind you, in fact following the edge of

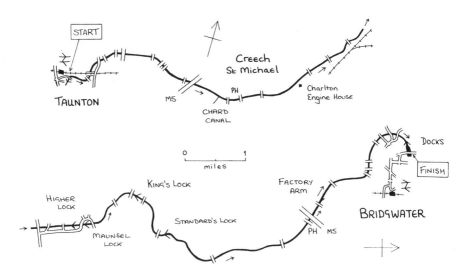

The Bridgwater & Taunton Canal

the present goods yard. This raised boats 19 ft from the B&T up to that of the GWC. The GWC was never a financial success and in 1853 was leased to the Great Western Railway. In 1864 the GWR bought the canal, only to close it three years later.

Start the walk along the right-hand bank. The tall GWR water tower to the left stands on some old limekilns that were supplied with both coal and lime from the canal. The water tank was also supplied from the canal. The B&T starts for Bridgwater by passing through an area of industrial works. At Obridge it goes under a pipe and then a railway bridge before swinging right to pass under a new road bridge and then Priorswood Bridge. This latter concrete structure is one of the last remaining obstacles to navigation between Taunton and Bridgwater. Fortunately, the replacement of the bridge is agreed in principle and there is even money allocated to the task. By 1993 the blockage should be lifted. At Bathpool the canal goes under the A38 and passes the St Quintin Hotel. You are now leaving Taunton behind and heading into the country. The last obstacle, it seems, is the M5 which you now go under. From here it is just a short stroll to the pleasant village of Creech St Michael. As the housing starts on the left side of the canal, keep an eye open on this side for an ivy-covered pillbox. Shortly after this is the site of the former junction with the Chard Canal.

The Chard Canal was opened in 1842 and closed just twenty-six years later. The 13½ mile long line was engineered by the relatively unknown Sydney Hall and comprised four incline planes, two aqueducts, three tunnels and two locks. At the time, Chard was an important wool and lace town and the canal carried 20–30,000 tons of coal p.a. to it. But 1842 was not a time to start building canals. Just four years after the opening of its new waterway, the company was considering converting it into a railway. This didn't occur and it was left to the opening of the Bristol & Exeter Railway's branch to Chard in 1867 to finally put pay to the Chard Canal. The line was bought by the Bristol & Exeter and closed in 1868. Not much remains now but here on the right are the buttressed walls of an embankment which carried the canal towards an aqueduct over the River Tone. At the junction there was formerly a stop lock, a towpath bridge and a lock-keeper's cottage, all of which have disappeared.

The B&T now heads through Creech St Michael and under Creech Bridge. The next two bridges, North End and Foxhole, were at one time swing bridges. Indeed, before two world wars there was a large number of swing bridges along the B&T. Most of these were destroyed during the war when the War Office, fearing a German invasion, converted the canal into a defensive fortification. It was this same move that produced all the fortified pillboxes and peculiar pyrimidal concrete obstacles that litter the entire length of the waterway, as indeed they do on the Kennet & Avon.

The canal now enters more open countryside. In 1/4 mile the towpath passes the large and partially derelict Charlton Engine House. This building, which dates from 1827, formerly housed steam engines which were used to

One of the curious things about the locks on the B&T is the fact that the ground paddle mechanism is fitted with a substantial counter-weight, the chain of which runs over the pulley to the paddle

pump water from the River Tone into the canal. From here the peace and quiet becomes even more intense and is only periodically destroyed by trains thundering past the Cogload Junction and Viaduct to the right. The canal meanwhile does a quick shimmy before going under the A361 (turn right here for the Railway Hotel pub) and past Black Hut Bridge (the black hut was formerly used by canal lengthsmen). After crossing an embankment the line reaches Higher Lock, Maunsel Lock and then King's Lock. The rise for each is about 5 ft 8 in. At King's Lock there is a rack of stop planks which are used to block off a section of canal in the event of an embankment burst or maintenance work. The groove for the planks is just above the upper gates. The canal has now circled round North Newton and returned to a northerly course to go through Standards Lock. One of the curious things about the locks on the B&T is the fact that the ground paddle mechanism is fitted with a substantial counterweight, the chain of which runs over the pulley to the paddle. This, with the reduction gear, makes operation of the paddle relatively simple. The next bridge is Fordgate Swing Bridge, a typical example of the type of bridge that predominated along the canal before the war. From here the line runs on to Huntworth Road Bridge and then onto Mead's Swing Bridge where the Boat & Anchor Inn sits in the shadow of the M5, which again spans the canal. Cross the canal at the next, Crossways, swing bridge. Before the completion of the Bridgwater Docks in 1841 this was the terminus of the canal. The original basin has been filled in

The tunnel-like Albert Street cutting in Bridgwater has, in the past, been subject to subsidence. The problem has now been stabilized but the walls still bear these massive supporting timbers

but was apparently close to a pillbox on the far side.

The canal is now approaching Bridgwater and the walk continues through Hamp, with a former brick pit (now a pond) to the left and the River Parrett to the right. The canal soon swings left, away from the river to go under three bridges, before bending back right to enter the tunnel-like Albert Street cutting. At one point it seems that only the huge wooden cross-buttresses stop the sheer cliff-like walls of the cutting from crumbling into the canal. From here it is a short stroll right through a cutting to Bowerings Animal Feed Mill and the much-redeveloped Bridgwater Docks. The docks were opened in 1841 and consist of two basins, the larger main one in front of you and a smaller outer one in the distance. Water from the tidal River Parrett was used to maintain water in the dock, which was separated from the river by the two locks on the far side. Thus the docks form a kind of floating harbour. The basin is being developed as a marina and, in theory, boats enter or leave it to the canal via the restored Newtown Lock.

Walk along the left-hand side of the basin and out to the road. Here it is possible to see the small outer (tidal) basin and the tidal gates and barge lock to the River Parrett. The tidal gates, which are now closed off by a concrete dam, could be used by coasters up to 180 ft by 42 ft but only those not exceeding 32 ft beam could then pass into the inner dock area. The barge lock measures 54 ft by 13 ft. Turn right cross the bridge, of a type known as a bascule bridge which is raised and lowered using a counterbalancing weight, and go round to Ware's Warehouse, one of the few original buildings still extant on the docks. To the right here is an original hand-operated crane. This is the end of the walk. To reach your return transport continue along the road to some traffic lights. Turn left over the River Parrett and then right to reach the bus station. For the railway station, walk past the bus station and through a car park. Then go along New Road and turn left along Eastover. Continue straight across the busy A38 and along St John Street. When this road bends right go straight on to reach the station.

Further Explorations

Having walked the entire length of the B&T, you may be fooled into thinking that there's nothing left to be done. There are, however, a surprisingly large number of canals in the south-west and the West Country branch of the Inland Waterways Association publishes a series of leaflets that describe walks along (among others) the Stover and Hackney canals, the Cann Quarry Canal, the Tavistock Canal, the Grand Western Canal, the Chard Canal and the Dorset & Somerset Canal. Perhaps the most historic of the canals in south-west England, however, is the Exeter.

The Exeter Canal dates from the time of Edward I, when Isabella de Fortibus, Countess of Devon, had a weir built across the River Exe, an act which forced boats to unload at Topsham where tolls were payable to – you guessed it – the Countess of Devon. Navigation was restored in 1290 but between 1317 and 1327 the river was filled in and further weirs built. It wasn't until 1539 that Exeter Corporation obtained an Act to render the river navigable. This wasn't very successful and in 1563 John Trew of Glamorgan was engaged to build a canal, the first to be built in Britain since Roman times. The Exeter Canal left the Exe near the city walls and ran to Matford Brook just below Countess Wear, a length of 3,110 yd. From there the river was improved to Topsham. It was opened in 1566 and cost £5,000. The canal had three pound-locks, the first on any British waterway, with vertically-rising guillotine gates. There was also a single pair of gates at the sea end. The canal wasn't easy to use: the approach was awkward, the line could only be entered at high tide and the river above Trew's Weir tended to silt up. In fact, by the end of the Civil War it was in a pretty bad state. As a result, in the 1670s the seaward end was extended 1/2 mile towards Topsham, a new entrance was built to take 60 ton craft and the rest dredged. Further improvements in the early eighteenth century meant that the canal could take coasting vessels and small deep-sea craft up to 150 tons. The three old locks were removed and the Double Locks built instead: a single lock of large size that served also as a passing place. There was still only a single pair of gates at the entrance, called Lower Lock, the sill of which was 4 ft below that on the Double Locks. There was also a pair of floodgates, called King's Arms sluice, where the canal entered the Exe.

The eighteenth century was one of great prosperity for the Exeter. Some 500 boats regularly used the line, shipping coal, slate, timber, woollens, cider, groceries and goods from southern Europe. In the middle of the century receipts averaged £747 p.a. and, by the end, £2,335 p.a. By the 1820s this profitability stimulated moves for further improvement. Under the control of James Green, the line was straightened and the rest dredged. Green also engineered the extension to Turf, 2 miles further down the estuary, where a proper entrance lock was built. At the same time the banks of the canal were raised so that it could take craft drawing 14 ft and carrying 400 tons. The cost of these improvements was £113,355 but the subsequent receipts increased considerably, reaching £8,550 in 1842–3. Coal imports increased and coal ships now entered the canal instead of unloading into lighters. Two ships a week arrived from London and there was both a coastal and a foreign trade. Goods could reach the capital in a week, although in bad weather it sometimes took a month.

The opening of the Bristol & Exeter Railway in 1844 had an adverse affect on trade and in 1846 the dues were reduced by a third. The Exeter

Basin was connected to the South Devon Railway from 1867 but traffic never recovered. By the turn of the twentieth century 275 vessels were still using the canal but receipts were down to £1,624 p.a. This level of traffic was sustained into the 1960s, 55,431 tons (mainly timber and oil) being handled in 1960. The last vessel to use the basin was the *Esso Jersey* which delivered oil to its terminal in 1972.

A walk of approximately 9½ miles starts at the Exeter Quay (OS ref: SX 923919 on Landranger 192). There is a car park near the National Maritime Museum. Alternatively, the quay can be reached from the centre of Exeter using the City Nipper bus G. The museum is contained within the warehouses on the quay on either side of the canal basin. The basin is 900 ft long, 17 ft deep and widens from 90 ft to 120 ft and was (and is) the Exeter terminus for the canal. Before starting it's well worth turning left to investigate the quay. Cross the River Exe by the blue suspension bridge (Cricklepot Bridge) and then turn right to cross the wooden Mallison Bridge. Here is a range of small shops and cafés as well as the headquarters of the Exeter Canal and Quay Trust in the wharfinger's house.

To start the walk, set off along the left-hand side of the Exe past the public conveniences and on past the Port Royal pub. Ahead on the river is Trew's Weir, built by John Trew to feed his canal, and across the river is the canal entrance with the single gates of King's Arms sluice, which gave boats access to the quay before the canal basin was built. Further on the path moves away from the river and passes between houses. Here turn sharp right to go over another suspension footbridge. This leads to a second bridge and then on to reach the canal. Turn left and walk along the towpath (note that there is towpath on both sides), past a swing bridge and on for about a mile to Double Locks. This massive structure (despite its name it is a single lock which replaced three separate locks in the early eighteenth century) is 312 ft long and 27 ft wide at the gates and is broad enough for two ships to pass. Charles Hadfield suggests that it is the largest manually operated lock in the country. Nowadays it is the only lock along the canal. Walk on past the Double Locks Inn, which dates from 1701. At Countess Wear the towpath crosses the busy A379 by passing, in short order, a power-operated lift bridge and a swing bridge. Shortly thereafter is Exeter sewage works and wharf. You may find moored here the vessel *Countess Wear*, a 265 ton sludge carrier that was built in Poole in 1963. This is the last commercial ship on the canal and it still makes regular trips to the sea where it dumps sewage sludge. After passing under the massive structure that carries the M5, the line moves on to the Topsham side lock. This was built to enable lighters and other small boats to move from the canal into the Exe to reach the town of Topsham. The lock has been derelict since 1976. Before the improvements made by James Green in the 1820s, the seaward terminus of the canal was above the position of the side lock, although it is not possible to determine precisely where. The final stretch of just over a mile leads on to the Turf Lock, the entrance to the canal, and the Turf Hotel. The lock was built on piles driven down through both the clay and underlying bog to the rock beneath. It cost £25,000 and was opened in 1830. The lock is 131 ft by 30 ft 3 in. Just above it there is a basin where larger vessels could tranship into lighters. It also acted as a temporary harbour where vessels could hold out for more favourable tide or wind.

To return to the quay, you can either cross to the opposite side of the canal and walk back along the other towpath, or you can continue along the sea wall into Star Cross where trains go back into town. If walking back, stay on the left bank of the canal to pass Trew's Weir and the Welcome Inn to reach the King's Arms sluice and the Maritime Museum.

Further Information

The Bridgwater & Taunton Canal is supported by the Somerset Inland Waterways Society which can be contacted at:

18 Lonsdale Road,
Cannington,
Bridgwater,
Somerset TA5 2JS.

The society has the objective of advocating the use, maintenance and development of all the inland waterways of Somerset.

The history of both the B&T and the Exeter Canal can be traced in:
Hadfield, C., *The Canals of South-West England*. David & Charles, 1967.

4
THE BUDE CANAL
Bude to Marhamchurch

Introduction

The Bude Canal is one of the oddest of the South's waterways. Situated in one of the least populated and least industrialized parts of the country, it appears to have no obvious chances of success. Yet here it was built and here it enjoyed a modicum of prosperity. The Bude was a curious mixture of conventional waterway and nineteenth-century inventiveness. The canal rode the hilly hinterland in a bold and uncompromising fashion. There are no fewer than six railed inclined planes on which the specially built tub-boats were hauled out of the canal and up the hills; an ingenious, if not necessarily reliable, solution to an otherwise intractable problem. And yet the prime cargo was nothing more extravagant than sand.

The canal begins, naturally enough, at Bude, a small town on the northern coast of Cornwall about 25 miles north of Bodmin. From there the line runs south to Helebridge where the first incline took the tub-boats up 120 ft to Marhamchurch. The canal then went east to Hobbacott, where the second incline raised the line by 225 ft. At Red Post the canal divided. On the northern arm, it crossed the River Tamar by the Burmsden Aqueduct and then took the Vealand incline up 58 ft to the summit level. Near Burmsden, the line divided again. One branch went up to the Tamar Lakes, the other continued to Blagdonmoor Wharf just north of Holsworthy. The southern arm from Red Post followed the course of the River Tamar south in the general direction of Launceston. The line is primarily downhill and thus takes in the Merrifield incline (a fall of 60 ft), the Tamerton incline (59 ft) and the Werrington incline (51 ft). The canal ends at Crossgate, just a couple of miles to the north-east of Launceston.

This wild, sometimes bleak, country is a real contrast to that which surrounds most canals. It is recommended to those who regularly walk the often wilder and bleaker inner-city stretches of the waterway network.

History

As every gardener knows, the acidity and physical make-up of soil greatly affects its fertility. Poor-draining, acidic earth won't produce good crops, let alone support the good life. The moorlands of Devon and Cornwall are therefore not promising places for farmers. Those who, in the eighteenth century, sought to establish farms on the plateaus of the region had a pretty lean time. The exceptions were the farmers who lived around the small, north coast town of Bude. For centuries the people who lived in the area dressed their soils with sand from the beach with miraculous results. The sand, with its high shell content and hence high calcium carbonate level, both neutralized the soil and improved its structure. The result was seen in better yields and richer farmers. At the appropriate time of year in the early 1700s, the beach at Bude was packed with people loading the precious 'manure' onto carts and wagons or into packs on mules and asses, which then took the tortuous and lengthy route home into the hills. The difficulties of doing this, and the wear and tear on the local roads, prompted thoughts of a more efficient system and attention focused on the prospects for a waterway.

It was John Edyvean who first suggested a Bude Canal. Edyvean, who had been building the St Columb Canal (near Newquay) for a similar purpose, proposed the line to a meeting in 1774. The original plan, surveyed by Edmund Leach and John Box, proposed to link the Bristol and English channels by rising up from Bude and passing over the moorland to join the River Tamar at Calstock, about 6 miles north of Plymouth. Although only 28 miles as the crow flies, the proposed canal ran for 90 miles, meandering around the contours. In this instance, a circuitous route was seen as advantageous in being able to reach the largest number of customers spread throughout the hinterland. Even this early proposal saw inclined planes as the most efficient way of raising loads up and down the many hills along the way. There were to be five, each consisting of trucks pulled along rails using specially designed engines. Goods would be transferred from the proposed small wooden tub-boats to the trucks and back again at every incline. The total building cost was put at £40,000.

The idea of the canal was welcomed by the local population and an Act to enable the construction was passed in 1774. However, by August 1775 enthusiasm seems to have cooled and nothing was started. In 1778 John Smeaton, who had been called in to pass comment, said that the hills and valleys of Cornwall weren't exactly an ideal place to build canals and estimated the cost of building Edyvean's line as nearer £119,000. To overcome this problem he drew up his own plans for a line between Bude and the

Tamar that was much shorter than the original proposal: 9¹/₂ miles to the Tamar with 15¹/₂ miles of river navigation to Greston Bridge, where the river would continue to Calstock. This was estimated as costing £46,109.

Further plans and estimates followed. In 1785 Edmund Leach resurveyed the original line and estimated a cost of £88,740. He also put some thought into the operation of the proposed inclined planes and pointed out that transferring loads from boat to truck and back again at each plane was cumbersome, time-consuming and costly. He proposed a boarded plane on which two cradles carrying the boats would run on dry rollers. The cradles were to be hauled up using a water wheel or men in a treadmill.

In April 1793 a local dignitary and inventor, Lord Stanhope, and some other local notables held a meeting to discuss a canal from Bude to Holsworthy and Hatherleigh. John and George Nuttall were asked to survey the route and reported on 25 October on a 75 mile long canal to carry 2 ton tub-boats. In this plan the Nuttalls included a proposal from Stanhope on the operation of the inclines. The small boats would be put onto wheels and pulled up the hill on rails using a horse. This design was later amended following a suggestion from Robert Fulton. The power to lift the boats, he suggested, could be obtained by adding water to a descending bucket. He

The American engineer and inventor Robert Fulton devised a water wheel-powered canal incline which he described in *A Treatise on the Improvement of Canal Navigation* (1796). A method derived from this was used on the Marhamchurch incline

British Waterways

also suggested that the boats themselves could be wheeled so that they could run up a short slope to drop into a huge tank or caisson which would then be pulled up the incline using the bucket-in-a-well system.

Like many projects proposed during the course of the Napoleonic War, the Bude Canal was put on ice for over twenty years. It wasn't until 1817 that James Green arrives in the history books. With the help of Thomas Shearn and the support of the new Lord Stanhope, he again surveyed a possible route. Green planned a canal on which tub-boats carrying 5 tons could be drawn along in groups of four by just one horse. The hillsides would be scaled using inclined planes which he reported as a third of the cost of locks, using a third of the amount of water and being five times quicker to use. The first 2 miles to Marhamchurch would take larger vessels. There the sand would be transferred to tub-boats to rise up an incline. One line would then go to Holsworthy and Blagdonmoor and perhaps even on to Okehampton. Another would turn south to Tamerton Bridge. A third line would run to Alfardisworthy, where a feeder reservoir would be built. The cost would be £128,341. Green suggested an annual toll revenue of £15,083, about 80 per cent of which would be derived from sand. A further £25,000, Green reported, would be needed to connect Tamerton Bridge with Launceston. Green also suggested that an extension of the Okehampton line to Crediton was feasible. With renewed enthusiasm an Act was passed in 1819 to give the newly formed Bude Harbour & Canal

Tub-boats in the canal basin at Bude. These simple vessels held 5 tons of sand and were moved up and down the inclined planes by means of wheels fitted to their hulls
British Waterways

Company powers to raise £95,000, with a further £20,000 if needed, to build a 46 mile line from Bude to Red Post, from where one route would go via Holsworthy to Thornbury (with branches to Alfardisworthy reservoir and Virworthy) and the other via Tamerton Bridge to Druxton. On 23 July 1819, with the ringing of bells and the gathering of 12,000 onlookers, Earl Stanhope laid the first stone of the breakwater and dug the first clod from the canal. This was followed by the consumption of 'ten hogsheads of cider and many thousand cakes'. Despite the occasional difficulty, by 8 July 1823 the harbour and canal as far as Tamerton Bridge were open.

The first weeks were encouraging. By May 1824 a hundred boats were reported to be on the canal and trade was brisk. Work on the line between Tamerton Bridge and Druxton was also underway. To finance this the

The beach and sea lock at Bude Harbour

company borrowed £16,000 from the Exchequer Bill Loan Commissioners (a kind of early job creation scheme). Two years later, however, it had to borrow a further £4,000. The final line was eventually finished in 1825, although the Blagdonmoor to Thornbury section was never actually built. The completed canal was just 35½ miles in length and the final cost was £118,000. There were six inclined planes: Marhamchurch, Hobbacott Down, Vealand, Merrifield, Tamerton and Werrington. Each had a double line of rails along which the tub-boats ran by means of small wheels fitted to their undersurfaces. Boats were drawn up the inclines by a chain which passed round a drum at the top. The power came from water: a bucket-in-a-well system at Hobbacott Down and water wheels everywhere else. When working, the planes were a great success. Unfortunately, virtually from the start they were prone to breakdown. Hobbacott's bucket system suffered numerous stoppages in its first year of operation due to the bucket chains breaking. Marhamchurch suffered from chain and gear wheel breakage. All the inclines suffered from broken tramrails. The canal generally had problems with leaks and slipping banks. By 1827, the repair and maintenance costs were still exceeding income from tolls. By 1830 the money available to John Honey, the resident engineer, was becoming tighter and he was often unable to do repairs or pay the labourers or taxmen. The farmers and traders were also complaining that the tolls were too high for them to ship sand at a profit. Indeed, many farmers had returned to collecting by cart. In 1831 tolls were lowered and trade recovered. By 1838 the canal was carrying nearly 60,000 tons p.a., 90 per cent of which was sand, and the remainder coal, culm, limestone, slate and building materials. The total revenue from tolls, harbour and basin dues and rents was £4,300, with expenses at £2,600. No dividend had yet been paid and the company still owed the commissioners £21,037 for principal and interest, and £3,200 of other debts. Despite the problems the beneficial effects of the canal were being felt. Sand at Launceston was now about 75 per cent cheaper than it was before the canal was built and land values surrounding the line were increased.

In 1838 a severe storm damaged the breakwater at Bude and it was rebuilt by the company. The funds to do this were raised by agreeing with the commissioners to divert trading surplus from the repayment of the loan to the repairs. Thus the debt to the commissioners increased further, but with trade remaining consistent it was reduced to £3,000 by 1864 and was repaid by 1870. Receipts peaked at £4,716 in 1841 and profits at £1,493 in 1859. But maintenance costs consistently made the operation of the canal uneconomic and forced the company to keep the tolls at rates which made the shipping of sand barely profitable. It was during the 1850s that the improvement in the roads and the introduction of artificial fertilizers began to impose themselves on the company's activities. And then the railways arrived. In 1865 the Launceston & South Devon Railway reached Launceston from Tavistock. In 1879 the South Western reached Holsworthy and in 1898 it was extended to Bude. The gradual incursion of competition from artificial fertilizers, imported along the railway, forced the canal company to reduce its tolls. By 1876 canal tolls were down to £1,897 (plus £152 in rent). But as maintenance costs were now low and the debt paid off, the first dividend was paid to shareholders at 10s. per share. It was to be the first of just eight paydays. By 1877 the success of 'artificial' lime meant that there was only one major customer left on the canal, Vivian & Sons. From 1878 sand-carrying went into terminal decline.

In 1884 Vivian & Sons decided to give up the trade and the canal company proposed to follow suit; an abandonment bill was proposed to Parliament. Although this was withdrawn and Vivians continued to use the canal for a time, the interest of the company increasingly focused on selling water from the Tamar Lake reservoir at Alfardisworthy to the towns of Stratton and Bude. In 1891 the Bude Harbour & Canal (Further Powers) Act enabled the company to close the canal from Marhamchurch to Brendon Moor, including the Druxton and Holsworthy branches, on 14 November. The plan was to maintain the length to the reservoir as far as the Hobbacott plane, from where water would be piped down to the towns. However, by 1894 the towns had been unable to raise any money and the scheme was dropped. By this time, large areas of the canal had been sold to local farmers. In 1895 the company tried, unsuccessfully, to sell itself to the London & South Western Railway. By 1898 the railway to Bude was open and canal traffic had virtually ceased. The end of the company came in February 1899, when agreement was reached with the Stratton & Bude Urban District Council to sell the remaining canal, including the Tamar Lake reservoir, for £8,000. This move was authorized by the Stratton & Bude Improvement Act of 1901 and the company formally changed hands on 1 January 1902. The line was finally abandoned as a waterway in 1912.

Most of the Bude Canal is now in private ownership, dry and undetectable. The two intact areas are the first 2 miles from Bude to Marhamchurch where, for some of the length, pleasure boating is allowed and the towpath open. This section is owned by the North Cornwall District Council. The second is the length from Venn to the Tamar Lakes reservoir. This latter section is not open to boats and is used solely to conduct water to Stratton and Bude. Virtually all of the rest has been bought by farmers or landowners and incorporated into fields. There is little chance of the Bude being fully restored, although the first 2 miles from the sea should remain open to the public. Other areas may, however, become more accessible, particularly after the recent formation of the Bude Canal Society.

The Walk

Start and finish: Bude (OS ref: SS 206064)
Distance: 5¹/₂ miles/8¹/₂ km
Map: OS Landranger 190 (Bude & Clovelly)
Car park: At Bude Wharf near Bude Castle and the library
Public transport: From BR at Barnstaple, take the Red Bus Company's no. 1 or 2 to Bideford and then no. 85 to Bude (enquiries: 0288-45444)

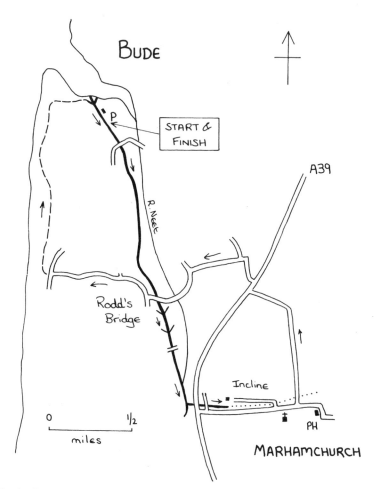

The Bude Canal

The walk starts at the Lower Wharf where there is a local museum in the Old Forge. The museum is open in the summer and contains various bits on the old canal, including a model of an inclined plane. The forge itself is just one of a group of old canal buildings that includes the harbourmaster's office, a one-storeyed stone building which has been used as a salt store, a tannery, a lime warehouse and other warehouse buildings.

To start the walk turn right towards the sea. Surprisingly there are still many remnants of the canal's heyday extant along the quay. On both sides there are mooring rings and on this side it is still possible to make out the rails of a 2 ft gauge tramway that leaves the wharf and goes down a slope to the beach. The railway was used to move sea sand up from the area around the nearby River Neet. The trucks were pulled by horses and then tipped into the tub-boats and barges moored at the quay. Originally the line had a 4 ft gauge but this was replaced in 1910. On occasions the shifting sands expose a turntable at the foot of the bridge. The tramway wasn't finally abandoned until August 1942. At the end near the lock there is a good view of the beach and the breakwater. The latter, built to protect both the harbour and the entrance to the canal, stretches north of Compass Point to Chapel Rock. It was built in 1838 to replace the original which had been washed away in a storm. The lock is a substantial structure: 116 ft long and 29 ft 6 in wide and able to take ships of 300 tons. Green's original plan was that barges 50 ft x 13 ft x 3 ft 6 in and able to carry 50 tons would be taken through the sea lock and allowed to settle on the beach as the tide went down. There they would be filled with sand, brought in again on the rising tide and towed to Marhamchurch.

Cross the canal via the lock gates and turn left to walk along the right-hand bank of the canal across the Company Wharf to Falcon Bridge, near the Falcon Hotel. Originally on this site was a swivel bridge which allowed ships to move from the lower wharf to the upper one (Sir Thomas Acland's Wharf, on the opposite bank just after the bridge). The present bridge severely restricts boat access to the rest of the still-extant waterway. Cross the road and continue along the left-hand bank of the canal. On the opposite side are the old lifeboat house and a renovated canal warehouse. The lifeboat house was built in June 1865 in memory of Elizabeth Moore Garden. It's altogether a peculiar site for a lifeboat house and the launching of the boat tended to damage Falcon Bridge. The large three-storeyed building was one of the first to be built on Sir Thomas Acland's Wharf. Sadly, a number of the other canal buildings have been demolished but once there was a shipbuilding yard, a sawmill, a steam laundry and a number of limekilns.

Continue past the winding hole and into more open country with the River Neet now running close on the left. Normally the barges were horse-towed to Marhamchurch, although at one time a steam-tug was tested. So much damage was done to the banks that it was soon withdrawn. The walk continues past a cast-iron milepost. Shortly after this, cross the canal via Rodd's Bridge. Walk on along the right-hand bank after passing through a gate. Within a short distance are the remains of Rodd's Bridge Lock, and a little farther along the one at Whalesborough. Both locks could handle barges and measured 63 ft x 14 ft 7 in. They have both been stripped down and their upper gates replaced by a concrete weir. The upper ground paddles are, apparently, still used to regulate the level of water in the canal to Helebridge. The pound between the two locks was recently dredged and the Bude Canal Angling Association intends to stock it with fish.

Above here the canal becomes more overgrown. After passing a small accommodation bridge the River Neet and the canal merge for a short distance. On the opposite bank is the weir over which the River Neet flows on its way to the sea. Continue out to cross the A39 and follow the path onwards. Cross the canal bridge and turn right to descend to the left-hand bank. From here you get a good view of the original Helebridge with its numerous rope score marks as well as Helebridge Wharf, which was the canal barge terminal. Goods were unloaded here either for storage and sale or transhipped onto tub-boats for passage further along the line. On the south side of the wharf is a small building which at one time was used for barge repairs and sailmaking. There is also a warehouse and the former home of George Casebourne, the company's engineer from 1832 to 1876. The cottages on the left bank of the wharf were formerly stables for the barge horses.

The path follows the north side of the basin to the bottom of the Marhamchurch inclined plane. Near the foot of the incline are the remains of Box's iron foundry (at which the canal's ironwork was cast). Bill Young tells us that the lintel over the end doors of the foundry is part of an old incline plane railway line. The incline itself, of which there is little trace, had a lift of 120 ft over a length of 836 ft. The tub-boats used on the canal from here on measured 20 ft long by 5 ft 6 in beam and were unique in having wheels fitted to the bottom. This enabled them to be pulled up the incline along rails. The motive power for the Marhamchurch incline was supplied by a 50 ft diameter overshot water-wheel which sadly no longer exists and would be almost impossible to restore without substantial funds. The mechanism was able to raise a boat in just 5 minutes using some 32 tons of water.

To reach Marhamchurch walk up the dirt track which runs to the left of the incline. At the top the track crosses the course of the canal (again with little to be seen) to reach the road. Turn left into central Marhamchurch. The return route starts at the Bray Institute. However, those desirous of lunch should continue straight on for a couple of hundred yards past a small shop to the Buller's Arms. To return, go back to the institute and take the turning which goes past a highly ornate chapel. On the right are new buildings and Old Canal Close, so-named because it was built on the canal bed. Now follow the road out to the A39. Turn right and then left towards Bude. This road bends left. When it bends back right, go straight on along a lane. At a T-junction turn left to go past the abutments of an old railway bridge, over the River Neet and then over the canal at Rodd's Bridge. The quick route back is to turn right here and return along the canal. The more exciting route is to carry straight on through Upton to the coast road. Here join the coastal path by crossing the road and bearing right. This obvious and well signposted route will take you back to the canal sea lock at Bude.

Further Explorations

Problems with access plague the rest of the Bude Canal. Many parts of it can, however, be seen from, for example, various road bridges. If you are interested in seeking out the remnants then Bill Young advises on what is to be seen if you have obtained permission from the landowner.

One route which isn't a right of way but is open for walkers through the good offices of the North Cornwall Council and South West Water goes along the Bude (feeder) Aqueduct to the Lower Tamar Lake. Ideally, the walk (which is 3 miles each way) is best undertaken with like-minded fellows who park at the Lower Tamar Lake (SS 294108 and well signposted from Kilkhampton) while you park in the tiniest of parking spaces at SS 288084, where a lane between Moreton Mill and Broomhill crosses the feeder.

Start along the left-hand bank from the lane bridge (Morton Bridge). The overgrown waterway was primarily built to act as a feeder from the reservoir to the main line and was never used extensively for navigation. It is still in water as it was bought by the Stratton & Bude Urban District Council on 1 January 1902 for use as a water supply for the two towns. The walk is along a cleared towpath through what must be some of the quietest and most peaceful countryside in southern England. The first half passes four bridges: Dexbeer, Gadlock, Wooda and Aldercott. At one point a wrecked mainte-nance tub-boat lies mouldering in its watery grave, only its wooden bones still showing above the vegetation. The canal shortly goes around a sharp bend before reaching Virworthy Wharf. This was formerly the limit to navi-gation. The canal buildings, a warehouse, a wharfinger's cottage and some stabling, have been renovated and are now private houses. The towpath from here on has been made into a waymarked trail from the lake car park. As part of the improvements the towpath sports some pleasant bronzes, the first of which is a representation of a tub-boat passing along the waterway.

A bronze on the towpath walk near the Tamar Lakes shows a train of tub-boats being towed along the Bude Canal

Continue over a lane, to the bottom of Lower Tamar Lake. The lower lake was built to supply the Bude Canal by damming the River Tamar. The upper lake, the dam of which can be seen in the distance, was built in 1975. Lower lake covers some 28 ha (about 70 acres) and holds 885 million litres (195 million gallons). Both lakes make good spots for picnicking and there are additional marked trails that go all the way round them. To complete this walk, however, cross the footbridge which goes over the large overflow weir and then turn left to the car park where, if you're lucky, your companion car can whisk you back to Morton Bridge. Otherwise, enjoy your picnic and then stroll gently back along the line.

Further Information

The Bude Canal Society has been formed to promote interest in and access to the waterway. The society can be contacted c/o:

Mrs Audrey Wheatley,

Tregea,

Lower Upton,

Bude,

Cornwall EX23 0LS.

The society holds regular meetings and publishes a newsletter.

Those interested in the history of the line should obtain a copy of:

Harris, H. & Ellis, M., *The Bude Canal*. David & Charles, 1972.

Driving tours of the rest of the Bude Canal can be found in the pages of:

Young, Bill, *Walking the Old Bude Canal*, published by Bill Young, Longmead, Diddies Road, Stratton, Bude, Cornwall EX23 9DW, 1991.

5
THE CHELMER & BLACKWATER NAVIGATION
Beeleigh to Heybridge Basin

Introduction

The route of the Chelmer & Blackwater Navigation from Chelmsford to the sea is the result of just over a century's worth of unseemly squabbling between two towns. The natural route would have passed along the River Chelmer through Maldon to the River Blackwater at Heybridge Creek and then simply down to the sea beyond Collier's Reach. But the most obvious routes aren't always those that result from man's complex political machinations.

The Chelmer & Blackwater Navigation starts in the centre of Chelmsford just $1/2$ mile south-east of the railway station at a spot called Springfield. From here the line goes almost immediately through Springfield Lock to join the River Chelmer and then heads east via Barnes Mill and Lock into the flat Essex countryside. The navigation now bends north on a new cut past Sandford Mill, before returning to an easterly course to the north of Little Baddow. At Ulting the tiny All Saints Church sits on the north bank among the trees. From here the navigation undertakes a southern loop to Hoe Mill before continuing on to Beeleigh, where the Chelmer meets the Blackwater at a waterway crossroads. While the combined rivers overflow south through Maldon, the canal continues in a south-easterly then a north-easterly direction, bypassing Maldon by taking a course through Heybridge. After returning to a south-east slant, a straight cut of over a mile ends at Heybridge Basin and the sea lock to Collier's Reach and the North Sea.

The result of the Chelmsford–Maldon feud is a fascinatingly contrived line and the wonderfully bewildering waterway crossroads at Beeleigh is worth an hour of anyone's time.

A boat-borne funeral procession on its way to Heybridge Cemetery along the Chelmer & Blackwater, *c.* 1905–10

Essex Record Office

History

The desire to make the River Chelmer navigable was established long before the age of canal mania. Andrew Yarranton, as long ago as 1677, proposed and planned the canalization of the 14 miles of river up to Essex's county town of Chelmsford. His plan, which included a survey and the brief for a Parliamentary bill, was well received in Chelmsford but was bitterly opposed by the people of Maldon. The main thrust of their concern was the inevitable loss of income from tolls, duties and wharfage if traffic passed them by on a direct route to Chelmsford. This opposition found favour among the owners and tenants of the watermills who were dependent on the river for their power supply. As a result the scheme, although innovative and far-sighted for its time, was dropped.

Nearly half a century later, on 13 and 14 July 1733, John Hore surveyed the river. Hore was an experienced navigation engineer from Newbury who had already worked on the Kennet, Stroudwater and Bristol Avon navigations. Hore proposed two schemes, the first to simply make the river navigable for £9,355, and the second to cut a wholly new navigation for £12,870. Despite the difference in cost, Hore favoured the latter as a way of avoiding conflicts with the landowners and millers. He justified this with a profit forecast of £382 p.a. However good an engineer he was, Hore had a reputation for being somewhat lax with finance. It was therefore relatively straightforward for those opposing the scheme to develop their own forecast with equal positiveness which predicted an annual loss of £430 10s. Again, the objectors proved powerful and the scheme was abandoned.

In 1762 the idea of a navigation was revived and surveys were carried out independently by John Smeaton and Thomas Yeoman. Both came up with a similar cost estimate; Smeaton's was £16,697. As before, the proposals were supported by Chelmsford, opposed by Maldon and had the same end result. But Chelmsford persisted. In 1765 Yeoman produced another plan and this was the basis for an application for a Parliamentary bill. Yeoman recommended widening the river at the surface to 30 ft and at the bottom to 20 ft with a depth of 4 ft. Locks were to be 70 ft by 14 ft 1 in. The cost estimate was £13,000. On the basis of Yeoman's plan, an Act was passed on 6 June 1766 'for making the River Chelmer navigable from the Port of Maldon to the Town of Chelmsford'. The navigation was to be built within twelve years but nothing was to be started until 25 per cent of the money was in hand. Thereby lay the end of this attempt, for despite numerous efforts it was found impossible to raise the necessary funds.

In 1772 yet another scheme was proposed, this time by an émigré Dutchman, Peter Muilman, at a meeting attended by various town dignitaries at the Chelmsford Coffee House. This plan was later amended to one in which a new cut from Maldon to Chelmsford was to be built, again with a view to avoiding problems with millowners. Muilman even offered to pay for the survey from his own pocket. However, all that actually came from the renewed excitement was another failure.

By 1792 canal mania was rearing its head across the nation. The success of inland navigation in other parts of the country and the increasing economic expansion during the period made the inhabitants of Chelmsford feel that they were losing out. A new proposal was launched with an observable increase in confidence. The plan took the navigation along the Chelmer to Beeleigh, where a new cut went away from Maldon to join the original course of the Blackwater which entered the estuary at Heybridge Creek. As this exit was perilously close to Maldon, an additional cut was proposed to leave the Blackwater at Heybridge and run for about a mile to a place now known as Heybridge Basin. From there a sea lock would give access to the estuary. This new line was surveyed by Charles Wedge under the direction of John Rennie. A further survey was carried out, again under Rennie's direction, in 1793 by Matthew Hall. Both surveys showed that by bypassing

Maldon the length of the navigation would only be increased by 2 miles to 13^1/$_2$ miles.

The people of Maldon were livid! They quickly published a pamphlet in which they alleged that the proposals were unsupported by evidence of public utility. For once, this opposition came to nought. The Act received Royal Assent on 17 June 1793 and established 'The Company of the Proprietors of the Chelmer and Blackwater Navigation'. The proprietors were authorized to raise £40,000 in £100 shares and a further £20,000 either by the issue of new shares or by borrowing. Tolls were set on a mileage basis, ranging from ^{1}/$_4$d. per mile per quarter of oats, malt and other grains, to 2d. per mile per chaldron of coal and 2^1/$_2$d. per mile per ton for other goods. Stone for roadmaking, other than for turnpikes, was to be carried free. The Act came into effect on 15 July 1793 and work began shortly thereafter. The project was nominally under the direction of John Rennie but was controlled on a day-to-day level by his assistant, Richard Coates, who had previously worked on the Ipswich & Stowmarket Navigation.

There were two main cuts: the stretch of 2^1/$_2$ miles between Beeleigh and Heybridge Basin; and the ^{1}/$_2$ mile from the river to the terminal at Springfield, Chelmsford. Altogether thirteen locks were built: from the Chelmsford end these were Springfield, Barnes Mill, Sandford, Cuton, Stoneham's, Little Baddow, Paper Mill, Rushes or Weir, Hoe Mill, Ricketts, two at Beeleigh and the sea lock. The Beeleigh locks were needed because the navigation diverged from the course of the Chelmer through a short cut to join the Blackwater, along which the line of the navigation continued before entering the final cut to Heybridge Basin. The Blackwater was diverted at this point into the Chelmer at Beeleigh Falls. The two locks at Beeleigh are therefore sited on each side of the present course of the Blackwater, providing protection at times of flood or drought.

By April 1796 work was sufficiently advanced to allow the lower part of the navigation to be used. On Saturday 23 April 1796 the brig *Fortunes Increase*, loaded with 150 chaldrons of coal from Sunderland, entered the line. The cargo was unloaded at a coal yard at Boreham and moved on to Chelmsford by road. The first load to be moved in the opposite direction left on 26 April, when a barge loaded with 150 sacks of flour departed from Hoe Mill for London. The final stretch to be completed was the cut from the river to the terminal basin at Chelmsford. This took another year. It wasn't until 3 June 1797 that coal barges arrived at Springfield Mead. As is usual with these things, they arrived in a grand procession with colours flying.

By the time the navigation was finished the cost had risen to £50,000. What was worse was that virtually immediately problems arose. In December 1797 serious flooding led to shoals in the river which impeded the movement of the barges. This problem got worse with every flood until 30 March 1799, when a meeting of the navigation committee resolved to send Lord Petre, one of the most important local landowners, to see John Rennie. Rennie was to be told that the committee had a claim on him to resurvey the navigation and suggest a cure for the defects without further cost. Rennie accepted responsibility, although his response implied that it was Coates who was really responsible. He carried out a survey on 25 May 1799 and remedial work was undertaken. By 1805 further problems arose when the millers at Moulsham, Barnes, Sandford, Little Baddow, Paper and Hoe claimed damages for the loss of water when their local locks were used, adding that the general condition of the locks was resulting in considerable leakage. Rennie was again called in and, following a survey on 25 November 1805, he suggested improvements at a cost of £4,918. In spite of these efforts the millers still seemed to be complaining in 1807.

Collier's Reach and the entrance to Heybridge Basin

Although there were these minor hiccups, on the whole the navigation performed well. Traffic was vigorous, even though in February 1799 the navigation froze over. Goods carried along the line included coal, timber, bricks, stone and general cargo inwards and grain and flour out. Success was such that in 1842 the line carried 60,000 tons of cargo. The barges used were 60 ft by 16 ft and could carry 25 tons. They were a special flat-bottomed type with a draught of just 2 ft. This was necessary to ensure good access on what was one of the shallowest waterways in the country. Some of the barges, which had no cabin accommodation, were apparently still horse-drawn until the 1960s. The cheap transport of coal into the area led to the establishment of a gasworks in Chelmsford in 1819, only the second to be built in Essex and the first inland. The navigation was also successful financially. Dividends were paid into the twentieth century and reached a peak of 5 per cent in the 1820s. In 1846 the original £100 shares were selling for £66, although by 1918 they were only worth £17 10s. The fall in both share value and dividend payment after 1838 was due, perhaps predictably, to the opening of the Eastern Counties Railway through Chelmsford in March 1843. But there is no doubt that the foresight of the original promoters helped Chelmsford grow from a small market town to the important centre that it is today.

After the Second World War the only traffic on the C&B was the carriage of timber to the sawmills and timber-yard of Gilbert Brown & Son Ltd, here photographed in the early 1900s

Essex Record Office

The C&B was never taken over by a railway company and, as a consequence, was not nationalized in 1948. The line remains independent and is owned by the Company of the Proprietors of the Chelmer & Blackwater Navigation Ltd. The navigation was in use commercially until 1972, although after the Second World War the only traffic was the carriage of timber to the sawmills and timber-yard of Brown & Son Ltd at Chelmsford Basin. The barges made the return journey empty. Gradually the proprietors are becoming aware of the leisure potential of this attractive waterway and have themselves started operating a trip boat during the summer. Following the 197th AGM in 1991 the proprietors viewed the line on board the cruise boat *Victoria*. The year had seen dredging work, the fitting of new lock gates, the extensive planting of trees and repairs to a listed building. The year also saw the first commercial trade for twenty years, when Blackwater Boats of Sandford Lock started to hire boats. The prospects for the navigation may therefore be bright and the line may yet play a part in the leisure time boating trade.

The Walk

Start and finish:	Langford (OS ref: TL 838090)
Distance:	7¹/₂ miles/12 km
Map:	OS Landranger 168 (Colchester)
Car park:	On road near St Giles Church, Langford
Public transport:	Chelmsford has a main-line BR station with frequent trains to London. Eastern National buses run to Langford and Heybridge (enquiries:0245-353104)

Facing away from the church, turn right to go past the old mill building for 50 yd. Just after Mill Cottage, and just before the Essex Water Company works, turn left to follow a footpath sign along a metalled road. The road bears left. Here the 'new' course of the River Blackwater can be seen to the right. The original course of the river ran further to the north-east via the mill at Langford. This 'new' river is therefore the overflow from the weir which became the main course of the Blackwater when the Langford mill was closed. The water to the left among the trees is not a river at all but is in fact a canal known as the Langford Cut. This was the only branch canal on the C&B and was originally called Mr Nicholas Westcomb's Navigation because it ran across his land to the mill at Langford. As it was entirely private it did not require an Act to sanction its construction. The line was surveyed in 1792 and opened for traffic in July 1793, about three years

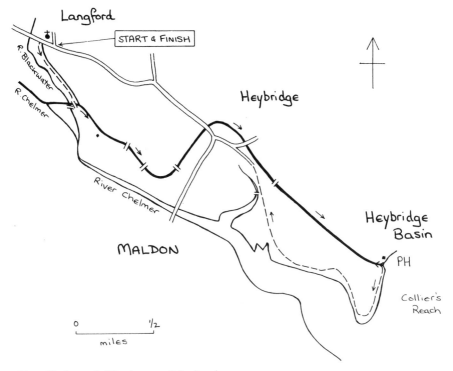

The Chelmer & Blackwater Navigation

before the C&B itself was complete. Originally the cut ran to join the Chelmer near Maldon, a distance of about a mile. It's now a little shorter as it joins the C&B at Beeleigh. The cut carried considerable traffic during the first half of the nineteenth century. By the second half traffic had all but gone and the last barge to reach the mill did so on 9 August 1881. The mill, which is actually not the original structure but a rebuild after a fire, closed in 1918 and was later purchased by the water company.

The route continues along the driveway to reach a bridge over a river. This is the Chelmer & Blackwater Navigation, a wholly new cut opened in 1796. To the left the Langford Cut peacefully joins the C&B. To the right is an extremely complex waterway junction that will need explanation. To get a good view, cross to the opposite bank and turn right. Walk up to the footbridge that passes over the weir and face upstream. Straight ahead is the new line of the River Blackwater that has flowed down from Witham, Braintree and beyond. To the left is the River Chelmer that has been rendered navigable (as part of the C&B) to Chelmsford. Behind you is the main downstream course of the Chelmer as it makes its way towards Collier's Reach and the North Sea. Flowing past you and on to the right is the new cut of the C&B on its way to Heybridge. This extraordinary complex is in fact a type of waterway crossroads. The main traffic lane went left–right, although water mostly still flows front–back. The flood weir that you are standing on is known as Long Weir and maintains the level of the canalized waterway. The original wooden footbridge that crossed the weir was built at the end of the eighteenth century, only to be washed away in 1947. If you continue for a short distance up the Chelmer you will see Beeleigh Lock, the last on the Chelmer portion of the navigation.

Return to the old brick accommodation bridge crossed earlier. Underneath it are the gates of Beeleigh flood lock. Walk on along a metalled lane with the C&B to your left. Opposite the entrance to Langford Cut and barely discernible on the right is the line taken originally by Mr Westcomb's pride and joy as it wended its way to join the River Blackwater. Those who purchase Pathfinder Map 1123 will see the course still marked.

To continue the walk, keep on the road until it bends right towards the Maldon Golf Club clubhouse. Bear left onto the grass to keep the navigation close left. At this point on the left-hand bank of the C&B it is possible to find a small stream entering the waterway. This was the original course of the Blackwater before the intervention of the mill at Langford. The C&B now follows the line of the river to Heybridge. The path eventually leaves the golf course behind some trees to reach a bridge. Cross here and turn right to follow the left bank. Go through a gate and to an old railway bridge. Here a new flood lock has been built. The path continues under the bridge as the navigation bends left. When I was here a complex rerouting of the right of way diverted the path left, over the railway bank and across a field on the opposite side. Whatever route you take, once around the corner, the waterway continues to a road bridge. Before reaching the bridge, note that a stream leaves the navigation from the right bank. This is the Blackwater wending its way out to sea via Heybridge Creek. From here on the C&B follows another new cut.

Bear left up to the road to Black Bridge. You are now in Heybridge. Cross the road and continue alongside the C&B, staying on the left-hand bank. The course bends right near Jeakins Crash Repairs and passes some old industrial units to reach another bridge (Wave Bridge). After crossing the road, continue down to the towpath on the left bank. The large factory building on the right-hand bank is William Bentall's agricultural engineering works or Heybridge Ironworks. Bentall built his factory here in 1804 to take advantage of the cheap land and the C&B which permitted the ready import of raw materials and the export of the finished goods around the world. In the nineteenth century this was one of the most important agricultural engineering firms in Essex. Among the implements exported from the works was the highly successful Bentall broadshare plough. The building on the canal bank was built in 1863 as a warehouse for the factory and is now a designated 'ancient monument'.

Continue into increasingly open country. At one point the route passes some entrance gates to the left. This is Beeleigh Cemetery, possibly the only one in the country to be served via its own canal wharf. Sadly the gates now look anything but pearly and clearly haven't been used for many a year. The canal, meanwhile, carries on along a straight course with numerous moored boats.

At the end of this section, about a mile from the road bridge, the navigation bends slightly left to reach Heybridge Basin. Opened in 1797, the basin has a tidal lock which gives access to the Blackwater estuary. It was built originally to hold sailing ships. Here the boats transhipped timber, coal and provisions to the broad, shallow-draught 25 ton barges which then travelled up the C&B to Chelmsford. A two-storey bow-windowed lockhouse flanks the entrance lock on the other side, a row of weatherboarded cottages and the Old Ship (formerly the Brig Inn and renamed in 1906) on this.

The sea lock was built to handle vessels up to 107 ft by 26 ft, allowing access for boats drawing 8 ft at neap tides and 12 ft at springs. The lock was lengthened after the Second World War to accommodate coasters that brought timber onto the C&B. If you continue to the far end of the lock, to see Collier's Reach and Northey Island on the far side, you may note that the lower gate of the tide lock is a type of caisson which slides sideways. It's electrically powered and chain-operated. Further round to the left is the Jolly Sailor pub. To continue the walk, cross the lower gate of the lock and go up to the sea wall embankment with the estuary to the left and a small lake (some old gravel workings) to the right. The town of Maldon can be seen to the right. Continue along the sea wall as it bends right with fine views of the Chelmer/Blackwater estuary and of an area of Maldon known as the Hythe to the left. The path eventually bends round, with Heybridge Creek (the original course of the Blackwater) to the left and some holiday huts to the right, to arrive at a minor road. Turn left and walk up to the main road. Turn right here past the post office and turn left just after Bentall's Mill to return back along the C&B to Langford. If in a hurry, when you reach Black Bridge it is possible to turn right to walk up the road to Langford (about 1 1/4 miles), although the original route is much more pleasant.

Further Explorations

· The stretch of canal between Maldon and Chelmsford makes for a fine 12 mile walk. Eastern National bus no. 31 runs between the two towns at roughly half-hourly intervals (enquiries: 0245-353104).

From central Maldon, walk along Silver Street which is to the left of All Saints Church. This goes past The Blue Boar Hotel and Maldon Court School to Beeleigh Road. Continue into a private road and then bear left along the fenced pathway. Continue straight on and across Maldon bypass. After this, go straight on to reach a field. Keep to the left edge and go over a stile. The path now passes Beeleigh Abbey. Continue along the drive to a T-junction. Turn right and follow the lane into Essex Water Company property. After Beeleigh Falls House, the driveway turns right. Here go left along a path and over a footbridge across the River Chelmer. After crossing, bear right and follow the path around to the C&B with the waterway crossroads to your right. Bear left to cross the C&B near Beeleigh Lock. Now turn left to walk along the right-hand bank.

The path winds through open country to reach Rickett's Bridge and Lock and then Hoe Mill Bridge, where the public right of way changes banks. Pass Hoe Mill Lock and then walk along the course of a new cut while the river takes a more southerly (and lower) route. The canal overlooks the river for a short stretch before the two rejoin near a substantial weir. From here the C&B turns north-west to Ulting where the delightful thirteenth-century Church of All Saints sits on the right bank with the churchyard descending to it. The navigation continues towards Chelmsford via Rushes Lock and under a footbridge. The next bridge is a road bridge and is followed by Paper Mill Lock, home of the C&B Navigation Company. Here you will

The diminutive navigation-side church at Ulting

also find Chelmer Cruises, which offers trips along the canal. At the next road bridge, Boreham Bridge, the footpath reverts to the right bank. After passing another small footbridge the C&B goes through Little Baddow Lock, where there is a fine mill pool and weir waterfalls. The line shortly turns abruptly left to Stoneham's Lock.

By this stage the tranquillity which has enveloped you since Maldon is disappearing rapidly. Turn left with the C&B to your left and the (relatively) new A12 on the right. After passing Cuton Lock, with its associated pillbox, and a small footbridge, go under the A12 and, step by step, peace is gradually restored. The towpath reaches Sandford Mill Bridge and Lock (from where Blackwater Boats operates) and then another small road bridge before bending right to Barnes Lock. The towpath continues over a small footbridge and into a field. Follow the course of the C&B round to the next road bridge which carries the 1932 vintage Chelmsford bypass.

The River Chelmer now heads south. You should follow the cut right to Springfield Basin. Just beyond the diversion is an old accommodation bridge and the last lock on the C&B (Springfield). At the end of the pathway the site of Chelmsford gasworks is still visible on the left. Brown's Timber Yard on the right of the basin is now occupied by Travis Perkins. To complete the walk, follow the path between the industrial sites to a road (Navigation Road) and turn left. This passes Travis Perkins and crosses Wharf Road to a T-junction. Turn left and walk on into central Chelmsford.

Further Information

The C&B is not operated by British Waterways but by its own company:
The Chelmer & Blackwater Navigation Company Ltd,
Paper Mill Lock,
Little Baddow,
Chelmsford,
Essex CM3 4BF.
Although there is no C&B society as such, the navigation has its supporters in the Chelmsford branch of the Inland Waterways Association. Those interested in finding out more should firstly contact the head office of the IWA in London. The address is given in Appendix B.

For those interested in the history of the canal, the following can be recommended:
Jarvis, S., *The Rivers Chelmer and Blackwater*. Lavenham Press, 1990.

6
THE GRAND JUNCTION CANAL
The Tring Reservoirs

Introduction

The state of the nation's canals in the 1950s can be no better demonstrated than by pointing out that the Grand Junction, or the Grand Union as it became, is the only canal in this book which would have survived in its entirety, excluding the branches, if the British Transport Commission had had its way. All the rest were considered as having 'insufficient commercial prospects to justify their retention'. The canal earned this respect because of its strategic position as the main canal line between London and the north. But fear not. The GJC has no conceit. You can walk along it just like any other mere mortal waterway and find it every bit as charming.

The GJC starts at Braunston where it forms a junction with the Oxford Canal, a prime route north to Birmingham and the Potteries. The canal then takes an easterly course through the Braunston Tunnel to its second junction at Norton where it meets the Old Union, the Leicester line to the River Trent. From here the GJC gradually turns south to pass Weedon and the Northampton arm at Gayton to Blisworth. The canal now goes through the Blisworth Tunnel to Stoke Bruerne. After passing the course of the Buckingham branch the line leaves Northamptonshire to enter Buckinghamshire via the Ouse Aqueduct near Wolverton. The former Newport Pagnell branch is passed at Milton Keynes as the line heads south to Fenny Stratford and Leighton Buzzard. The Aylesbury arm meets the canal at Marsworth near the Tring reservoirs. From Berkhamsted the canal goes through Hemel Hempstead and Watford to Rickmansworth and Uxbridge. After passing the Slough arm, the canal bears east through London's suburbs to reach Bulls Bridge, from where the Paddington arm heads into the centre of the city. The main line, meanwhile, reaches its southerly end when it joins the River Thames at Brentford.

A stroll around the Tring reservoirs provides a fine varied walk with plenty of canal interest, bags of wildlife and a good pub. Need more be said?

History

One of the key objectives of canal developers in the late eighteenth century was to provide a navigable link between London and the Midlands. That initial connection had been made with the completion of the Thames & Severn Canal which, with the Stroudwater Navigation, joined the rivers Severn and Thames for a journey from Birmingham to London of 269$\frac{1}{2}$ miles. Just a year later, the opening of the Oxford Canal reduced that distance to 227 miles. However, neither line was exactly direct and both were subject to the vagaries of navigation on the upper Thames, which was often flooded in winter and drought-ridden in summer. As a consequence, even though London was no longer isolated from the industry and minerals of the North, a shorter, less-troublesome route was still a key objective.

A more direct waterway from Braunston on the Oxford Canal to London was first planned at the end of 1791. The proposed line to Brentford, known at that time as the Braunston Canal, would undercut the Oxford route by 60 miles and be both quicker and more reliable. Prospects for trade were good and had been recently bolstered by the completion of the Coventry Canal between Atherstone and Fazeley, thereby giving access to

Edward Powell's horse-drawn pair *Water Lilly* and *Forget Me Not* at Braunston Top Lock in 1913 with his and a friend's families posing for the camera

British Waterways

the Trent & Mersey Canal. Goods and minerals from Birmingham, Manchester, Liverpool and the Potteries could all now reach Braunston and, it was proposed, would wish to take the new line to London. By early January 1792 the plan was being so widely discussed that canals were being planned to form junctions with the proposed line. The Old Union was promoted in February 1792 to join the new canal. This would feed traffic to and from Leicester, the Trent and the Derbyshire coalfields. The Warwick Canals to Birmingham and Stratford were planned with the new London route in mind and provided the prospect of a much shorter route to Birmingham. The only people against the whole idea were, not unnaturally, the Oxford Canal Company. As soon as plans for the new canal became apparent, the Oxford decided to back an alternative route, the London & Western, or Hampton Gay Canal to run from Hampton Gay, 6 miles north of Oxford, to Isleworth via Thame, Wendover, Amersham and Uxbridge. For a while the Hampton Gay drew support but it couldn't fight the sheer inevitability of the much more direct route and the scheme soon disappeared into obscurity.

The first survey for what was becoming known as the Grand Junction Canal was made in 1792 by James Barnes who, ironically enough, had previously worked on the Oxford. This was followed by a second survey by

The New Mill on the Wendover arm near Tring was once wind-powered, as this 1900 photograph shows

British Waterways

William Jessop in the autumn. Although the two routes were broadly similar, the southern section which was originally to run from Watford via Harrow to Brentford was diverted via Uxbridge. The main engineering efforts were identified as being in the high ground at Braunston, Blisworth, Tring and Langley Bury near Watford, and in the provision of water to the summits at Braunston and Tring. The canal was to be a broad line of 90 miles, able to take barges capable of carrying 70 tons.

The GJC received its Royal Assent on 30 April 1793 with powers to raise £600,000. The Act, and a subsequent one in 1794, detailed branches to Daventry and Watford (although neither was actually built), Northampton (to meet the Old Union), Buckingham, Aylesbury and Wendover. Among the promoters of the new canal were the banker William Praed, the Marquess of Buckingham, the Duke of Grafton, the earls of Clarendon and Essex, the Earl Spencer and the Hon. Edward Bouverie. Later the company coopted numerous MPs; in 1812 five were on the company's board. These dignitaries gave the company a lot of political clout, a situation that didn't exactly enhance its popularity. With the passage of the Act, Praed was made chairman, Jessop was appointed chief engineer and James Barnes was made resident engineer.

Work began almost immediately at both ends of the line. By December 3,000 navvies were reported to be at work. The cutting of Braunston and Blisworth tunnels was a priority and they were started straight away. At the southern end building began at Brentford, where the line used the River Brent as far as Greenford from where it ran east to the River Colne, which it then followed to Watford. This southern end of the canal was open to Uxbridge on 3 November 1794. Meanwhile at Braunston problems arose when the line was discovered to run through quicksands, but by 21 June 1796 the tunnel was open and the canal finished from Braunston Junction to Weedon. In the south, the end of 1797 saw the line reach Hemel Hempstead. This included the construction of some highly ornamental sections through Cassiobury and Grove parks near Watford. The southern works reached Tring in 1799 and Fenny Stratford on 28 May 1800. By September the southern line was open to the bottom of Stoke Bruerne Locks and trade was possible over the whole canal except for the tunnel at Blisworth.

The completion of the work to this point was only possible with the provision of extra funds. The company obtained an Act in December 1795 which allowed it to raise a further £225,000. This still wasn't enough. Further Acts, in 1798, 1801 and 1803, raised an additional £150,000, £150,000 and £400,000 respectively. The cost of the canal was by now was approaching four times Jessop's original estimate. It was Blisworth Tunnel that was proving to be the GJC's Achilles heel as various sections collapsed. At one stage Jessop suggested building twenty-nine locks over the hill but

Barnes, supported by Robert Whitworth and John Rennie, called in as consultants, proposed a new tunnel on a slightly different line. A brief financial hitch meant that the work couldn't start until the autumn of 1802 so a temporary toll road was built instead. This was later replaced by a double-track tramroad which ran from Blisworth Wharf to the bottom of the Stoke Bruerne Locks. The new tunnel, built with underground drainage channels to prevent subsidence, was finally completed on 25 March 1805 and with this the whole canal was open for traffic. As opened, the GJC main line was $93^{1}/_{2}$ miles long with 101 locks. The branches brought these figures to $136^{3}/_{4}$ miles and 137 locks. The cost to the end of 1811, i.e. without either the Northampton or Aylesbury branches which had still to be built, was £1,646,000.

The decision to go ahead with the branch to Northampton proved problematical as the GJC waited to see whether the Old Union Canal would go there. It didn't and the people of Northampton forced the GJC to build a line, initially a tramway but later a 5 mile canal branch from Gayton Junction, opened on 1 May 1815. The line to Aylesbury was only built after the Marquess of Buckingham had insisted. It was completed in May 1815. One through line that was built independently of the GJC was that from Napton to Birmingham. This line was composed of two separate canal companies, the Warwick & Birmingham and the Warwick & Napton. These were both opened in 1800 and provided the GJC with a more direct route into Birmingham. Meanwhile, at the London end another branch was added following an Act passed in April 1795. The new line went from the GJC at Bulls Bridge, Southall for $13^{1}/_{2}$ miles to Paddington. This important extension was opened on 10 July 1801. At Paddington Basin warehouses and wharves were built and it soon became a busy terminus. A further extension along Regent's Canal followed in 1812.

As soon as the main line was operational the GJC held meetings with its neighbours in order to convince them to widen their canals and thus improve carrying efficiency. This far-sighted scheme was supported grudgingly by most but some, such as the Oxford, were positively hostile. The issue was complicated by the proposal in 1796 for an entirely new broad waterway, the Commercial Canal, to join the rivers Dee, Mersey, Trent and Thames. The project received wide support and the GJC was seemingly relieved when the scheme was defeated in 1797. However, the increasing financial stringency of the moment was also enough to shelve any further canal-widening schemes. Indeed, it was then seen that there were advantages in two narrow boats being able to pass each other in Braunston and Blisworth tunnels.

The traffic along the GJC in the early part of the nineteenth century was highly promising. The company was able to pay a 3 per cent dividend for the year after the canal opened, when toll receipts totalled £87,392. Even though coal taken into London faced a ban and then a tariff, as part of a protectionist scheme for the existing merchants, coal transport rapidly became the single biggest business. The Canal Act of 1805 allowed 50,000 tons p.a. to be shipped into Paddington on payment of duty. Later this limit was removed and gradually the tariff, 1s. 1d. a ton in the 1830s, was reduced so that by 1890 it was abolished completely. But in 1810, 109,844 tons of inland coal and 22,209 tons of sea coal was carried. By 1821 these figures had increased to 149,004 and 39,804 tons respectively. But it was the enormous range of different cargo which was so impressive. Pig iron, for example, was brought from Shropshire and Staffordshire into the city for manufacturing, together with castings and pipework. Some 24,364 tons were shipped in 1801 and this grew to 55,694 tons in 1840. There was a steady trade in bricks, timber and lime (77,797 tons in 1810). Agricultural produce was brought from all around the Midlands and there was a busy hay, straw, vegetable and cattle market at Paddington. On top of this, there was salt from Cheshire, glass from Stourbridge, pottery from Staffordshire, manufactured goods from Manchester and Birmingham, and stone from Derbyshire and Yorkshire. Exports from London included groceries, raw materials and products from overseas, together with ashes, cinders and manure. In total in 1810, some 343,560 tons of cargo were shipped in or out of London, a figure that does not include cargo shipped locally. One of the surprising things about the figure is the relative equality of the north–south trade: 191,696 tons going south; 151,864 tons going north. In 1813, receipts reached £168,390 and the company issued a 7 per cent dividend.

Despite a few minor ups and downs trade continued at this level throughout the 1820s. In 1827, for example, receipts reached £187,532 from tolls and a 13 per cent dividend was paid. But as early as 1824, the outlook changed when John Rennie was asked to carry out a survey for a London–Birmingham railway. The canal companies held a meeting in November, where it was decided to have a joint study on the future of the railways and to evaluate ways of upgrading the canal lines. Despite this action the mere threat of a railway caused GJC share values to fall from £350 in 1824 to £225 in 1831. Luckily any further action on the London & Birmingham was in abeyance because of a financial crisis. This gave the GJC a chance to rationalize its toll schemes and to investigate the potential for using steam to haul boats. It was also able to consider ways of fighting the new railways. However, its campaign did not receive the support of the other companies and the Railway Act was passed in May 1833.

In 1835 the canal carried 192,859 tons of trade to London and 631,815 tons of local traffic. Improvements were made, including the doubling of the flight of locks at Stoke Bruerne and the building of new reservoirs at Tring. Despite good business, the prospect of competition from the railways meant that tolls were reduced in January 1837. Thus marked the start of the steady decline in receipts from the peak of £198,086 in 1836. On 12 November 1838 the London & Birmingham Railway was opened to Euston and because of the need to reduce tolls just to compete, receipts on the GJC dropped instantly. By 1842, earnings were down 43 per cent on the 1836 level. This was despite a steady growth in the amount of cargo carried. More cuts were announced in 1857, following discussions with the London & North Western Railway and the Great Western Railway and an agreement designed to maintain differentials. This arrangement was such that it allowed a small rise in tolls in 1859 but it did not prevent virtually the entire coal-carrying business, the prime activity for the GJC, being lost to the railways.

In an attempt to rekindle business, the company decided in 1848 to start its own carrying company. This it did by raising £114,550 in preference shares. The company also started to use steam cargo-carrying boats, usually with a butty in tow. These were uniquely unpopular with the other canal companies who claimed that they were being sailed too quickly and too recklessly. Such recklessness included the carrying of explosives and one incident with a GJC steamboat at Macclesfield Bridge on the Regent's Canal in 1874 led to claims totalling £80,000 and eventual withdrawal from the carrying business in 1876. Steam engines were also installed in the Blisworth and Braunston tunnels to tow boats through. By 1871 steam tugs were employed in the tunnels, a service that continued until 1936.

In the mid-nineteenth century income was falling but the amount of cargo carried was not. Through tonnage, i.e. not including local traffic, stood at 294,141 tons in 1845. However, by 1870 the steady decline in trade was becoming apparent, with just 135,657 tons being shipped to and from the capital. It is perhaps surprising therefore to find the GJC spending £107,000 in 1883 to build a new 5 mile long branch to Slough, a town more than adequately served by the GWR (although this turned out to be a highly profitable venture). The GJC responded to the general downturn by trying to form an 'amalgamation' of all the interactive canals in the south and east Midlands. With the development of various jealousies and factions, this brave attempt failed.

The GJC was obviously not defeated by this failure for soon after the company inspected the Grand Union and Old Union canals (the Leicester line), and made a series of suggestions on ways of improving and increasing the traffic. The Leicester line companies replied by offering to sell, a deal that was eventually agreed on 12 July 1893 (completed on 29 September 1894) – the Grand Union for £10,500 and the Old Union for £6,500. With prompting from the canal carriers Fellow, Morton & Clayton Ltd, the GJC set about dredging its new possession and improving some of the bottle-necks, such as the Foxton and Watford locks. The purchase also stimulated the negotiation of agreements with the Leicester and Loughborough navigations and the Erewash Canal for lower through tolls.

Despite this expansion the dawn of the new century was not a promising one for the GJC. More and more traffic was being lost firstly to the railways and then to the roads. Unusually for canal companies, the response of the GJC and the Regent's Canal was to enter into a period of collaboration. In 1914 the two companies formed a joint committee of directors and, after the First World War, the companies decided to merge. To do this the Regent's bought the GJC to form the (new) Grand Union Canal Company. This was achieved on 1 January 1929 at a cost of £801,442. The new company then bought the Warwick Canals for £136,003. The grouping was further expanded in January 1932 when the Leicester and Loughborough naviga-tions and the Erewash Canal were also purchased for a total of £75,423. An agreement to purchase the Oxford Canal, however, fell through for various technical reasons. For the first time the inland waterway line from London to Birmingham and London to the Trent was under one roof.

The new Grand Union was committed to expanding the use of the water-way. The key parts of its plan involved making the canal to Birmingham suitable for barges and providing an improved design of barge to work it. The improvement budget for 1931 amounted to one million pounds (with the help of a government guarantee). One key area for improvement were the Hatton Locks north of Warwick which were all broadened. The com-pany also (re)started its own carrying company by buying Associated Canal Carriers Ltd, and renaming it the Grand Union Canal Carrying Co. Ltd.

The history of the company after this period of hopeful growth is one of disappointment. Receipts were falling rather than increasing and the hoped for traffic never arrived. No dividends were paid on ordinary shares between 1933 and 1945, and in 1948 the company was nationalized and put under the control of the British Transport Commission (later British Waterways). Because of its strategic importance as the prime route between London and Birmingham, the Grand Union was never in the same kind of danger as other canals. Indeed, in the Report of the Board of Survey in 1955, the line was listed as one of the few 'Waterways to be developed'. The line suffered a slight demotion in the 1968 Transport Act in not being listed as a com-mercial waterway. However, it is considered to be a cruising waterway and is thus as well protected as any of the nation's canals can be.

The Walk

Start and finish: Tring BR station (OS ref: SP 951122)
Distance: 7¹/₂ miles/12 km
Map: OS Landranger 165 (Aylesbury & Leighton Buzzard)

Car park: At Tring station or on road near canal bridge
Public transport: Tring BR from London Euston or Rugby

Tring station can be found off the A41 Berkhamsted to Aylesbury road to the north of the dual carriageway Tring bypass. It is well signposted from the main road. Access to the canal is from a road bridge that is 200 yd south (towards central Tring) of the station. Go down the steps to the right of the road and start the walk along the right-hand bank.

The GJC reaches its 3 mile long southern summit here at Tring, at some 400 ft above sea level. The builders reached Tring in 1799 and the resultant cutting is 1½ miles long and 30 ft deep. It took five years to dig! Remember that the navvies at the time had just spades and wheelbarrows with which to do the job. The cuttings on the Birmingham & Liverpool Junction Canal at Woodseaves and Grub Street are deeper but Telford designed and built the B&LJC in 1825–35, by which time engineering techniques had advanced considerably.

The towpath changes sides at Tring Cutting Bridge and then continues for a further ½ mile before the sides of the cutting subside. After passing through a short zigzag, you arrive at some mooring spaces, a winding hole

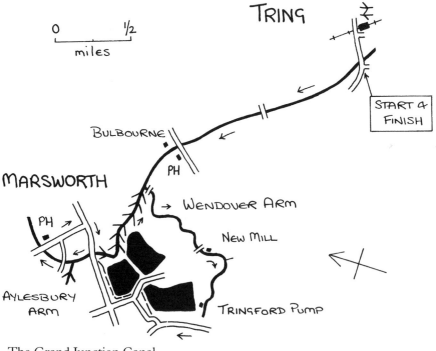

The Grand Junction Canal

and Upper Icknield Way Bridge. If craving refreshment, the appropriately named Grand Junction Arms pub can seen on the road. The walk, meanwhile, continues under the bridge and past British Waterways' (formerly the GJC's) Bulbourne maintenance yard, a collection of rather fine Victorian buildings, one of which has a rather ornate tower. Towpathers who have ventured north to see the remains of the Foxton inclined plane on the Leicester line near Market Harborough may be interested to know that the GJC built a small incline here in 1896 to test the idea before building the real thing.

The path now meanders past a picnic site to reach further mooring spaces, some cottages and Bulbourne Junction. Here is another BW maintenance yard, including a dry dock and a lengthsman's cottage. The GJC main line goes straight on through Marsworth Upper Lock. We, however, go under the roving bridge to turn left along the Wendover arm. The Wendover branch canal, originally $6^3/4$ miles long, was authorized by an Act of 1794 and was finished in 1797. Its prime function was to act as a spring-fed feeder for the GJC main line, although the people of Wendover might have disagreed. The central section, which leaked badly, was largely unused by 1897 (when it was shown to be losing more water than it was adding) and abandoned in 1904. Today the arm from the GJC runs for just $1^1/4$ miles. At one time it looked as if the people of Wendover would be more adequately served by a main line: the London & Western or Hampton Gay Canal would have passed this way *en route* between the Oxford Canal at Thrupp and Uxbridge. The idea was well received and, at the height of canal mania in 1792, attracted considerable financial support. The scheme disintegrated in what appears to have been a wall of non-cooperation. In the end, the GJC guaranteed the Oxford annual receipts of £10,000 p.a. and the latter dropped the whole idea. In the event the Oxford never needed to ask the GJC to top up its earnings.

The Wendover branch feels both narrower and more remote than the GJC main line. The towpath changes sides at the first bridge (Gamnel Bridge) and continues alongside Heygates flour mill or New Mill. Although many of the buildings here are of relatively recent vintage at least two show their age with canalside loading bays. The line continues to pass the Tring feeder, one of the original small streams that fed into the Wendover arm and hence into the GJC. Within a short distance the arm reaches Tringford pumping station. The vast reservoirs that you will see shortly all feed to the station which then delivers the water into the Wendover arm and thus into the GJC. Observant towpathers will notice the feeder delivering the precious supply into the canal just opposite the main building. The Boulton & Watt engine started its work in August 1818. It was joined by a second engine, the York engine, in 1839. Since 1913 the task has been carried out by electric pumps originally powered by diesel generators.

The towpath continues to reach the remains of a lock where the current line comes to an end. Walk up to the bridge (Little Tring Bridge) to see the remains of the dry section and then turn right along the road. After ¼ mile take a right turn. Within a short distance you will pass a house on the right and the lane will bend left. Turn right over a stile and across a field to another stile. This path then leads left through some scrub and out to Tringford reservoir. As mentioned, the three reservoirs here provide the vital supplies needed to keep the Tring summit in water. They are interconnected by culverts to Tringford pumping station. The first reservoir on the Tring summit was built in 1802 on what was formerly the site of a marsh. That reservoir, Wilstone, is about ⅔ mile to the south-west (left) of here. It fed the canal via a pump which lifted water into the Wendover arm. This was supplemented in 1806 by the Marsworth reservoir, ahead to the right of centre beyond the road. In 1811 Wilstone had been expanded but this still wasn't enough. The reservoir in front of you, Tringford, was opened in

Tringford pumping station on the Wendover arm

1816, and in the following year Startopsend, the water to the centre-left, was added. The reservoirs were all fed from small streams, run-offs and even from Tring sewage works. Despite these efforts, by the 1830s the water shortage was becoming critical and the GJC was forced to impose severe restrictions on lock use: boats could only go through locks in pairs or face an extra toll. To avoid this, Wilstone was again expanded. Yet there were still problems during 1902 when water was so short that only 80–90 boats a week were allowed to pass to and from the summit, compared with 130 normally. This led to huge queues. Boats, crews and horses are reported to have littered the banks of the canal, each awaiting its turn. The reservoirs now form a National Nature Reserve for wintering wildfowl.

The footpath passes over a weir. Continue straight on and out to a minor road. Bear left down to the next reservoir, Startopsend. Bear left here and along the straight edge of the embankment. This turns 90 degrees right and on to a British Waterways car park near The Angler's Retreat pub. Take the steps that go down left through the car park and out to the road. Cross the road to The White Lion pub. Cross the bridge (the Lower Icknield Way Bridge) that goes over the GJC and turn left to go down to the right-hand bank of the canal. Within a short distance the canal reaches Marsworth Junction. Here on the left is the entrance to the Aylesbury arm.

This branch was opened in 1815, some ten years after the completion of the GJC. It descends by sixteen narrow locks for a total distance of 6¼ miles. The first lock seen from the GJC is, in fact, a staircase of two, i.e. it is two locks which share a centre gate. At one stage it was thought that the Aylesbury may be extended westwards to bypass the upper Thames. Two different schemes were proposed. The first, the Western Union Canal, ran from Cowley on the GJC to Maidenhead or Marlow and so to the Kennet & Avon. This disappeared under a weight of objections from the Thames Commissioners and various landowners. The second plan, the Western Junction Canal, would have taken the line via Thame to Abingdon on the Thames near the entrance to the Wilts & Berks Canal. This was authorized in 1793 but failed to interest the GJC which didn't believe that it would deliver any traffic. Only after the intervention of the Marquess of Buckingham was a line built at all and then only as far as Aylesbury. It never was extended to Abingdon. The walk from Marsworth to Aylesbury is described in a leaflet available from BW. The return trip is by bus (enquiries: 0296-23445).

Continue along the main line (a signpost here promises Braunston in 54¼ miles) and past a BW wharf and office on the left-hand bank. The towpath changes sides at the next bridge. It is then just a short distance to the following bridge where you leave the canal by turning right along the road. The Ship, on the canal just beyond the bridge, was once a pub but is now a small shop. The road goes into Marsworth village and on its way it passes The Red Lion pub (recommended in CAMRA's *Good Beer Guide*) and continues past a school and a small grocery store. At the T-junction, turn right and follow the road back to the bridge near The White Lion.

Cross over the canal and turn left to take up the towpath on the right bank. This leads to a lock. The double-arched bridge here seems an oddity but in fact dates back to the time when the locks along this stretch were all paired. Originally the locks were built wide to handle barges. However, they were commonly only worked by narrow boats and consequently used excessive amounts of water. To curb this waste, boats were forced to use the locks in pairs or pay extra, a move that was hardly popular with either the boat owners or their crews. In 1838–9 narrow locks were built alongside the broad locks and thus the amount of water wasted was reduced. Only later, as water supplies improved and engined boats began to tow a butty, were the narrow locks filled in.

After passing to the left of the third Tring reservoir, Marsworth, the canal twists and turns on its way up to Bulbourne Junction, picking up a series of locks as it goes. There are seven altogether between Startop's End Bridge and Bulbourne, a rise of 40 ft to the Tring summit. Again, as part of the measures introduced to conserve water, the Marsworth Locks were each built with side ponds where water from an emptying lock could be run into them and then back to partly fill the lock the next time it was filled. Along this stretch are also two fine lock-keeper's cottages. The towpath eventually returns to Marsworth Top Lock and the BW dry dock at Bulbourne Junction. Cross the Wendover arm by the bridge and walk on to the Bulbourne depot, then back to the starting point at or near Tring station.

Further Explorations

The towpath of the Grand Union Canal is due for wondrous things. British Waterways has plans to make it into a long-distance footpath between Birmingham and London (Gas Street to Paddington). This, the first National Waterway Walk, should open during 1993 to coincide with the 200th anniversary of the GJC Act. As part of the launch, an official guidebook will be published. However, you don't have to wait. Many riparian councils have published leaflets which describe towpath walks. Those interested should enquire of local authorities, tourist information offices, libraries or BW at Watford.

At the northern end of the GJC, there is a pleasant short stroll of 3 miles around the famous canal junction of Braunston (OS Landranger 152. OS ref: SP 537662). The village is just off the A45 between Daventry and

Rugby. Park in the High Street near the post office and start the walk by continuing along the road to a bus shelter. Bear right past a factory (National Starch & Chemical Ltd) and then turn right along a lane to reach The Admiral Nelson. Keep to the left of the pub and walk on to Anchor House. Bear right to reach the canal at Braunston Top Lock. Cross the small accommodation bridge and turn left past the lock cottage and on to reach the western portal of Braunston Tunnel.

They had quite a lot of problems building Braunston Tunnel. Quicksands led to subsidence and then they discovered that the line through the hill wasn't built straight so that there's a distinct kink in the middle. It was opened in 1796 and is 2,042 yd long. In the early days the tunnel was worked by 'leggers', men who lay on the deck of the boat and pushed it through by walking against the roof or the side of the tunnel. The horses, meanwhile, went over the hill via a country path. In 1870 the company tested a system in which moving wire ropes were used to pull boats through. The idea wasn't terribly successful and was replaced a year later by a steam tug.

Return to Top Lock and walk along the canal to pass three more locks and then The Admiral Nelson, built in 1730 and thus here long before the GJC. Two locks further on, you reach Bottom Lock where The Boat Shop sells provisions and other canal ware. Just beyond the shop is the old pump house. This formerly contained a steam engine which moved water back up the Braunston flight into the summit pound. A little further on, Braunston Marina to the left is situated on what remains of the old reservoirs.

Continue over the Horseley Ironworks Footbridge and on past Butchers Bridge to reach a second Horseley Bridge. This second channel marks the former course of the Oxford Canal. Before the construction of the GJC, the Oxford Canal came through Braunston to reach this point, before turning left on its meandering way to Banbury. When the GJC was built the two formed a junction here. Those coming from London could turn left for Napton (where there is a further junction for Birmingham via the Warwick Canals) or go straight on for Hawkesbury (where the Oxford joined the Coventry Canal). The building ahead of you along the canal is the Stop House where tolls were collected and craft were registered before crossing the junction. When the Oxford was improved in the 1830s, the junction was moved and a highly convoluted length of canal bypassed. This reduced a 2³/₄ mile long stretch to just ³/₄ mile. You will see the new junction shortly. Most of the old waterway has disappeared into the fields but this short starting section now forms part of the boat-yard.

To see the new junction, continue past the Stop House, now a BW information centre, and then under the A45 road bridge. The new junction really is magnificent with not one but two Horseley iron bridges crossing a triangular canal entrance. This is the northernmost end of the GJC and the canal to the left and ahead is the Oxford. To the left is the route to Napton and ahead the line to Hawkesbury. The start of the southern Oxford is marked by another fine bridge, this time a brick one. This is a turnover bridge. Here the structure has its ramps built facing the same direction so that the barge horse can change canal sides without needing to disconnect the towrope.

To complete the walk, pass under the A45 for a second time before reaching the next bridge. This you have to climb up to in order to cross the canal. Continue over a stile and into a field. Walk up the hill, keeping the hedge close left to reach another stile opposite the church. Walk on to a road junction and turn left to return to the post office.

Purists will dislike the canal at Stoke Bruerne (OS Landranger 152. OS ref: SP 743499). The village must have more double-yellow lines than the rest of Northamptonshire put together and the canal has The Canal Museum, a shop, a café, a pub and swarms of people. Despite that, the museum is worth a visit and the canal itself has plenty of interest. A quick stroll north along the Tarmaced towpath takes you to Blisworth Tunnel, the

The canal at Stoke Bruerne

sixth-longest canal tunnel in England at 3,056 yd. The current tunnel was in fact the second attempt. The first, about 130 yd to the right of here, was abandoned before it was finished following a series of collapses. All in all it took twelve years to find a way through the hill (it was opened in 1805) and cost the company £90,000. As at Braunston, the tunnel was originally worked by leggers. Over the years the tunnel has continued to have problems with subsidence and, in the early 1980s, it was closed for four years for repair. Four million pounds was spent on relining the structure. A small display of the concrete blocks used is laid out near the tunnel entrance. The buildings near the portal were once a small stable and a maintenance workshop. Back at the museum, the Stoke Bruerne Locks still bear the marks of the time when the GJC attempted to speed passage by 'doubling up'. The old lock is presently home to an old boat-weighing machine. This peculiar mechanism was used on the Glamorganshire Canal when toll collectors wished to check the loading of a narrow boat as it passed a toll point. If you continue under the bridge, it is possible to stroll on to see the five remaining Stoke Locks and the pump house at the foot of the flight, which was used to return water back into the top pound.

Further Information

There is no Grand Junction or Grand Union Canal society as such but there is a Grand Junction Region within the Inland Waterways Association. It has branch secretaries at High Wycombe, Welwyn Garden City, Northampton and Milton Keynes. The address and telephone number of the IWA can be found in Appendix B.

The fullest historical account of the GJC is contained in:

Faulkner, A.H., *The Grand Junction Canal.* David & Charles, 1972.

7
THE KENNET & AVON CANAL
Bradford-on-Avon to Bath

Introduction

It is hard to believe that just a decade ago the Kennet & Avon was a derelict mess. Today the waterway is a superb amenity and a splendid sight. It is living proof that restoration of these so-called lost canals is not only possible but thoroughly worthwhile. The K&A is rich in wildlife, fine architecture and great scenery. Coupled with the fact that it's readily accessible and makes for good walking along the entire 86^1/$_2$ miles, it rivals any in the country.

The eastern end of the K&A starts at Reading, where it joins the River Thames. From this junction the former Kennet Navigation passes through the county of Berkshire to Newbury where the K&A 'cut' begins. After Hungerford the canal enters the rural charm of Wiltshire. Here are some of the line's greatest technical achievements: the oldest beam engines in operation at Crofton; the Bruce Tunnel at Savernake; and the magnificent flight of Caen Hill Locks at Devizes. From the headquarters and museum of the Canal Trust at Devizes, the path continues to Bradford-on-Avon. The way between Bradford and Bath passes through some great scenery and presents some more of the canal's wonderful history: two fine aqueducts and the fascinating water-powered Claverton pumping station. At Bath the canal joins the old Avon Navigation to pass through Saltford and Keynsham to reach the tidal Avon at Hanham Mills. From there the River Avon runs through the centre of Bristol and out to the sea.

This is as fine a route as you'll find in any walking book (let alone this one). It has regular public transport, loads of things to see, convenient and pleasant pubs and two fine towns at either end. It should be enough to tempt the staunchest of armchair towpathers out into the fresh air.

Claverton pumping station

History

By the time canal mania swept the nation, the idea of building a waterway to link London and Bristol was already nearly 200 years old. In 1626 an Oxford don, Henry Briggs, carried out a survey and suggested that if the River Avon was made navigable to Malmesbury and the Thames to Cricklade, then a short length of canal could link the two. How seriously the idea was considered is hard to assess but after the Civil War no fewer than five separate bills were introduced to Parliament, none successfully.

With the more visionary scheme dropped, it was left to two local developments to get the ball rolling. In 1699 Bath Corporation revived a plan of 1606 to make the Avon navigable from Bristol. Although there were objections, including claims that it would 'prejudice the Health of the Bath', the requisite powers were obtained on 22 May 1712. However, with further protest, the idea was shelved. Meanwhile, in 1708 a bill to make the River Kennet navigable from the Thames at Reading to Newbury was brought before Parliament. Supported by the towns of west Berkshire and Wiltshire, and fought vigorously by the people of Reading who feared loss of trade, the Act received Royal Assent on 21 September 1715. John Hore of Newbury engineered the line which followed the river via a series of artificial cuts. The 18½ mile long Kennet Navigation was opened in 1723 at a cost of £84,000.

By this time Bath was a major spa town and many of its fine buildings were under construction. The advantage of being able to import building materials along a new waterway became ever more apparent and objections to the 1699 scheme subsided. In 1724 the corporation assigned its interest in the river to the 'Proprietors of the Navigation between Bath and Hanham Mills' and employed John Hore as engineer. The work proceeded well and on 15 December 1727 the first barge reached Bath loaded with deal, pig lead and meal. The new line had cost £12,000. The Avon soon became an important waterway. Bath stone was exported around the country and coal came from Shropshire. There were also boats which for a shilling took passengers between Bristol and Bath in just four hours. At a meeting in Hungerford in March 1788, a line was discussed for a project then called the Western Canal which would join the Kennet and Avon Navigations. A second meeting, on 16 April appointed three engineers (Messrs Barns, Simcock and Weston) to carry out a survey. In the summer of 1789 they reported on a route that went from Newbury to Hungerford, Ramsbury, Marlborough, Calne, Chippenham, Lacock, Melksham, Bradford-on-Avon and Bath. After some discussion concerning the practicality of this line, John Rennie was asked to resurvey the route and advise. On 3 November 1790 he reported that the route was fine and the meeting resolved unanimously to proceed.

Raising funds proved harder than expected but with the arrival of canal mania prospects improved. In January 1793 Rennie was asked to undertake a detailed survey. He reported in July that a more southerly line through Hungerford, Great Bedwyn, Devizes, Trowbridge and Bradford was preferred as the water supply to the original route was suspect. The revised plan was approved at a meeting in Marlborough on 27 August 1793 with the cost estimated as £377,364 (including a branch to Marlborough that was never built). With this plan the committee, under the new name of the Kennet & Avon Canal, presented its bill to Parliament and received Royal

Boats at Mytchett on the day of the re-opening of the Basingstoke Canal, 10 May 1991

Albert Street cutting on the Bridgwater & Taunton Canal

May blossom on the Royal Military Canal at Appledore

The eastern portal of Sapperton Tunnel near Coates on the Thames & Severn Canal

Cleveland House and Sydney Gardens on the Kennet and Avon Canal

Residential boats on the Regent's Canal near Little Venice

The canal basin on the Bude Canal

British Waterways' Bulbourne depot on the Grand Junction Canal

Assent on 17 April 1794. The Act, for a 55 mile long canal, authorized the raising of £420,000 by 3,500 shares and the powers to raise a further £150,000 by mortgage should it be needed. Charles Dundas was appointed chairman and Rennie engineer. One of Rennie's first decisions was to build a wide (50 ton barge) canal rather than a narrow boat line. Some small alterations to the route were also made: Trowbridge was bypassed and the line at Crofton altered to reduce the length of the Savernake Tunnel. By October 1794 work had started at both Bradford-on-Avon and Newbury.

Generally the building of the K&A was harder than expected for business, geological and constructional reasons. The inexperience of many of the contractors, coupled with the largely unknown geology, inevitably meant that the work was more costly and more time-consuming than originally estimated. Furthermore, the Napoleonic Wars were having an adverse affect on the economy as a whole, causing inflation and reducing confidence. The company had problems raising funds and shareholders got behind with their payments. Despite this, in 1796 the K&A Company bought up virtually all of the Avon Navigation shares (one remained in private hands until 1885). This had the benefit of providing a cash flow.

By April 1797 the financial situation was such that the committee, following pressure from its bankers, instructed Rennie to reduce the works. Its position wasn't helped by the fact that the company treasurer, Francis Page, had secreted over £10,000 out of the accounts. To pay back the sum, Page and his brother offered to sell the Kennet Navigation to the K&A but were turned down, presumably because the company was short of ready cash. By 1799, with the canal open at the eastern end to Hungerford but with the western end inaccessible, the committee was forced to virtually halt the work. By December 1800 things looked grim. The line was still not ready and there was little hope of raising any funds to complete it. Only with the release of 4,000 new shares, after the passage of an Act in May 1801, was money forthcoming. This allowed the work to continue, if slowly, so that by 1803, with a grocer, John Thomas, acting as the resident engineer, the canal was open from Bath to Foxhanger, near Devizes (although there was no connection yet with the Avon) and from Great Bedwyn to Newbury. By 1804 Rennie had to report that although he had already spent over half a million pounds, it would still need an extra £141,724. A new Act of 1805 permitted a further injection of funds which were used to complete the central section and to start the Crofton pumping station and Wilton reservoir, both essential if the summit level was to be kept in water.

By 1809 virtually the entire line was ready, with only the flights of locks up Caen Hill to Devizes and down from Bath to the Avon still to be finished. With yet another Act passed on 3 June 1809 to raise a further £80,000, the final works were completed. On 28 December 1810 a barge-load of stone ascended the Caen Hill Locks and, without any ceremony or celebration, the line was open. It had, with the purchase of the Kennet Navigation in 1812, cost a total of £979,314.

Over the next thirty years the K&A was a success. It regularly returned profits and dividends and was constantly busy. The cost of shipping goods from London to Bristol was reduced by half, with a journey time for a horse-drawn boat of ten days (the 55 miles from Newbury to Bath took 3½ days). Later, with the use of high-speed fly-boats, the London–Bristol time was reduced to just five days. Over half the business at this time was coal coming from the Somerset Coal Canal, which joined the K&A near the Dundas Aqueduct at Monkton Combe. A large proportion of this went north along the Wilts & Berks Canal which left the K&A at Semington for Swindon and the northern Thames. Plans for similar linking canals were manifold and included a line to the Basingstoke Canal, more direct routes to Bristol and London, proposals for a new line to Salisbury and the Dorset & Somerset Canal which would have run from Bradford to Sturminster Newton. None of these projects were completed, the initial enthusiasm dying as the reality of canal-ownership dawned in a post-canal mania world.

The other reality that was to dawn was that of the railway. A line from London to Bristol was proposed as early as 1824. Luckily for the K&A, its arrival was delayed until 30 June 1841, when the Great Western Railway

Dundas Aqueduct at Combe Hay

linked the two cities. When the line finally opened, virtually all the through traffic was lost to the railway and the K&A's annual receipts fell from £51,173 to £39,936. To compete the company cut wages and made economies and was thereby able to reduce tolls: for instance, by 25 per cent in September 1841. It made no difference. Indeed, more railways were built, including, in 1848, a line that ran alongside the canal from Reading to Pewsey. Further toll reductions were made in order to sustain business. The lack of success of this move meant that by 1851 the company was unable to pay a dividend. In 1852 the end came. The GWR Act no. 1 allowed the railway company to take over the canal in its entirety. The interest of the GWR had started in 1845 when the canal committee had sponsored a review as to whether the canal could be converted into a railway. Immediately the GWR, fearing competition, made enquiries and was rebuffed. The K&A played hard to get for a while, even introducing a bill to Parliament for the London, Newbury & Bath Direct Railway in 1846. After the rejection of the bill, the company agreed to the sale on 18 March 1851 and this was enabled by an Act of 30 June 1852.

Despite the various legal constraints on the GWR forcing it to keep the navigation open, it paid no real attention to the canal, which gradually fell into disrepair. Trade declined from 360,610 tons in 1848 to 210,567 tons in 1868. The railway company's attitude to its canal subsidiary is amply reflected in the decision in 1864 to move the administration of the waterway to offices in Paddington, 34 miles from Reading. By 1877 the canal made a loss of £1,920 and profits were never seen again. Many of the canal-carrying companies filed claims against the GWR with the Board of Trade. C. Evans & Co., for example, complained about the lack of dredging along the line which rendered some parts difficult, if not impossible, to navigate. Despite the complaints and despite a Board of Trade report which confirmed that there was a problem, the GWR remained unconvinced by canal transport and allowed the line to continue its steady decline.

By 1905 annual traffic was down to 63,979 tons, a decline stimulated by the fact that tolls on the K&A were 50 per cent higher than on any comparable waterway in the country. By this time the canal was beginning to suffer from chronic water shortage. The closure of the Somerset Coal Canal and the Wilts & Berks meant that two important sources of water had been shut off. Improved land drainage also meant that there was limited surface water run-off. As a result many stretches, such as the 9 mile pound near Bath, were often difficult to navigate. The GWR's official view in 1905 was that railways were much more efficient and that there was little value in improving the canals. Following the First World War, increased levels of road traffic gradually took the rest of the business. In October 1926 the GWR announced that it proposed to close the entire line from Bath to Reading. This it would do by shutting all the locks (often by converting them into weirs) yet maintaining water levels. It was further suggested that local authorities should take control of that portion of the line that ran through their boroughs. The level of objections was such that the plan was withdrawn.

After further managerial re-organization in 1932, traffic declined to very low levels, with only the occasional pleasure launch ploughing through the weed. By the time that the railways were nationalized in 1948 the canal was only barely passable. From its poor post-war state, it fell into complete dereliction: locks fell apart, whole sections dried out. Eventually, in 1954 the BTC planned to close the canal (other than the Avon section). The response, at a time when the canal preservation movement was beginning to gain ground, was significant. The K&A branch of the Inland Waterways Association was one of the first to be formed and it soon led to the setting up of the K&A Canal Association to lead the fight against the planned closure. In 1955 the BTC Board of Survey put the K&A into category three of its report, namely 'Waterways having insufficient commercial prospects to justify their retention'. In the subsequent Act, the BTC was relieved of responsibility for maintaining the canal. The situation was rescued by the Bowes Committee in 1958. Although it saw no justification in raising the status of the K&A, it recommended that the line be considered for redevelopment. In 1962 the Inland Waterways Redevelopment Advisory Committee proposed that the canal be restored, albeit with little government cash, and that the canal association be allowed to play a role. With this the association became the K&A Canal Trust Ltd and the period of fund raising and restoration began.

It is the trust that has been the driving force in the revival of the K&A's fortunes over the last thirty years. From modest beginnings it has worked hand in hand with British Waterways and others to gradually bring life back to the canal. It is one of the great restoration achievements, which was officially recognized on 8 August 1990 when the Queen re-opened the canal. Once again it was possible to navigate from London to Bristol by way of the K&A canal.

The Walk

Start:	Bradford-on-Avon railway station (OS ref: ST 824606)
Finish:	Bath railway station (OS ref: ST 753643)
Distance:	$9^1/_2$ miles/$15^1/_2$ km
Maps:	OS Landranger 173 (Swindon & Devizes) and 172 (Bristol & Bath)

Return: Badgerline buses 264/265 from Bath stop at the Avon Bridge in Bradford and run regularly (enquiries: 0225-464446)

Car park: Well signposted at the railway station and in town

Public transport: Walk starts and ends near BR stations

From Bradford-on-Avon town centre, go along Frome Road towards Frome for 1/4 mile, past the Canal Tavern to reach a bridge that goes over the canal. On the left is Bradford Upper Wharf and the relatively deep (10 ft 3 in) Bradford Lock (no. 14). The first cuts of the K&A (as opposed to the river navigations) were made here in October 1794. Upper Wharf has a slipway and a dry dock which was formerly used as a gauging station where the carrying capacity of boats was assessed and tolls calculated. The stone wharfinger's house has been converted into a trust shop and the building also houses toilets. If visiting on a summer weekend, it may be possible to take a trip on the trust's narrow boat *Ladywood*.

To start the walk along the 'nine mile pound' (there being no locks between here and Bath) it is necessary to return to the Canal Tavern. Take

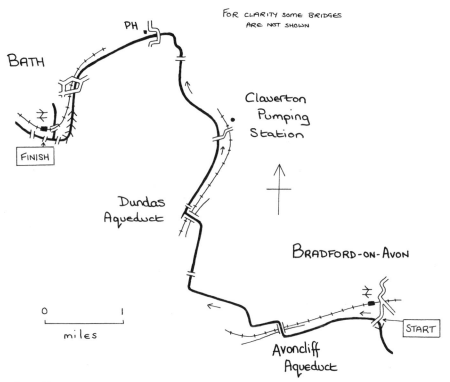

The Kennet & Avon Canal

the path that goes down the side of the pub to reach Bradford Lower Wharf and the canal. The towpath is on the right-hand bank. Within a short distance the canal bends left and passes a park, at the end of which is a fine fourteenth-century tithe barn. The course then curves away from the railway and the River Avon and passes Bradford-on-Avon Swing Bridge. The wooded hill to the left (Becky Addy Wood) was once the site of a quarry from which stone was brought down to the canal by means of a tramway. Within 1/2 mile the canal reaches Avoncliff where, after some buildings, the canal turns sharp right to Avoncliff Aqueduct. This is the first of two fine stone aqueducts along this section of the waterway. Built of local limestone, it was started in March 1796 and finished two years later. The poor quality of the stone caused the structure to crumble almost immediately and it is now much patched with brick and, in the 1980s, was substantially reinforced with concrete. This means that the sag in the centre of the span isn't as serious as it looks. The railway arrived over half a century later and led to the addition of the slightly less flamboyant extension on the northern side. In cold weather stalactite icicles reputedly hung from the ceiling of the aqueduct, making a significant hazard to passing trains. Railwaymen were employed to break them off every morning.

Before continuing to Bath, the towpath changes sides. Turn right to go down the slope towards the Canal Bookshop and the Cross Guns pub. After

Avoncliff Aqueduct in the 1950s. It was later restored

British Waterways

about 5–10 yd turn left to go under the aqueduct and then up the steps on the left. Here is Teazel's Coffee House and a towpath sign pointing to Dundas. Cross the aqueduct and turn left. The canal is now on the side of Winsley Hill and you can look down through the trees to the River Avon. This section is grounded on a type of oolite limestone which is highly liable to subsidence, making the canal bed prone to 'blowouts'. The problem was so great that the whole length was dry from 1954 until the early 1980s. The stretch was restored by firstly lining the bed with polythene and then covering it with concrete. The frequency of the landslips prompted the company to install a series of emergency stop gates (eighteen in 7^1/$_2$ miles) so that any given length could be isolated and repaired as quickly as possible. Over the years most of the gates have been replaced with stop planks (you'll see them in stacks all the way along the route) but stop gates are still in position on either side of the Dundas Aqueduct.

The canal straightens with some scrubby hedging to the left. Amid the undergrowth, down the slope towards the Avon, is Avoncliff Stone Wharf. These overgrown ruins are all that remain of the wharf for the Becky Addy Wood stone. In former times a railed way ran from the quarry across the aqueduct to end here, where the stone was transhipped onto barges.

Shortly, the canal turns right to Winsley Bridge. During the First World War convalescing soldiers stayed at the nearby Winsley Hospital. As part of the recuperation, they were given boat rides to Bradford and back using the Red Cross' narrow boat *Bittern*. After a gentle bend left, the canal passes through Murhill. Here, in the early 1800s, a tramway connected the wharf to Winsley quarries on the hill above. The path continues along a straight stretch for about ^{1}/$_2$ mile through woodland to Limpley Stoke Bridge. The view to the left through the trees goes across the valley to the River Avon, the Viaduct Hotel and the line of narrow boats that are moored in the Bath and Dundas Canal Company marina. After a bungalow and a derelict building, a lengthsman's cottage and barge horse stable respectively, the canal passes through a stop gate and turns sharp left. On the right bank is the former Conkwell Quarry Wharf but the attention is grabbed by the Dundas Aqueduct which takes the canal from the east side of the valley to the west before it swings west into Bath.

Charles Dundas was the first chairman of the canal company and memorial plaques to both him and John Thomas, a superintendent of works, were added to the aqueduct in 1838. Building work started here in August 1796 and, as at Avoncliff, stone from the company's own quarries was used. John Rennie preferred brick but was overruled by his committee. In the event Rennie was proved right. The Conkwell Quarry stone may have been handy but it was not of good quality and soon started to crumble. As a result, some rebuilding was needed virtually straight away and the aqueduct took nine years to finish. Despite this, it's a beautiful structure. When built, it had three arches and spanned 150 ft. A further arch was added at the western end when the railway opened. As at Avoncliff, extensive renovation was needed when the canal was restored and the rejuvenated aqueduct was re-opened in July 1984.

Cross the aqueduct to a footbridge. The narrow waterway on the left is the mooring site for the Bath and Dundas Canal Co. It was once the terminus of the Somerset Coal Canal. The SCC opened in 1805 to carry coal from the thirty or so Somerset collieries. The line ran from here to Midford where it split, one branch continuing to Timsbury via Combe Hay and Dunkerton, the other to Wellow. At Combe Hay the SCC carried out a series of trials with a boat lift which was capable of lifting a narrow boat 70 ft in just two minutes. The system relied on keeping a tank watertight, a challenge that proved beyond the technology available. It was eventually replaced with a flight of twenty-two locks. The SCC went into liquidation in 1893 and was converted into a railway. Ealing comedy fans will know the route as home to *The Titfield Thunderbolt*. Sadly, it closed in 1951.

All that remains of Dundas Wharf is a crane and two stone buildings, the left-hand one a tollhouse and the other a small warehouse. Go past the wharf crane and left of the old stone warehouse to Dundas Bridge, where there is another pair of stop gates. Cross the bridge and turn left to continue along the path on the right-hand bank. The path continues past Millbrook Swing Bridge and on to Claverton Road Bridge. Here you take a short diversion. Bear right down Ferry Lane to a railway crossing and then a small bridge. On the left is a millpond and the Claverton pumping station. This is a true wonder. The site was formerly home to a grist mill and was leased by the K&A when it was realized that water supplies to this end of the canal were insufficient to guarantee continuous navigation. A new building was put on the site and the pump, designed by John Rennie, was finished in 1813. It consists of a large waterwheel 18 ft in diameter and 25 ft wide, which is driven by the River Avon. The wheel powers two beams and pumps and lifts water 47 ft up to the canal at a rate of 100,000 gallons per hour. When the K&A was still a commercial concern, the pump worked twenty-four hours a day. Subsequently it was worked less and less, and in 1952 a log entered the works causing a jam which sheared off some of the wooden teeth from the pit wheel, so that it stopped working altogether. This splendid water-powered pump was then replaced by diesel power and left to gently rot. However, the K&A Canal Trust have, with the help of Bath University, restored the pump into full working order. If you're here on a summer weekend you may be able to see the pump operating (check with the Canal Trust for times). During the rest of the week, water is pumped using electricity.

Return to Claverton Road Bridge and turn right along the canal. Within a few yards the delivery leat from the Claverton pump pours water into the canal. The towpath continues under Harding's Bridge and on to Hampton

Wharf and Bathampton Swing Bridge. The canal does a double bend and passes Canal Farmhouse. The towpath now goes through a gate to reach Bathampton Primary School before going under Bathampton Bridge and out to a small green near the George Inn. The front door of the George originally opened where the canal now stands and was moved to its present position when the canal was built. The building itself dates from the fourteenth century and was originally part of Bathampton Priory.

The stretch from Bathampton to Darlington Wharf is a straight 1¼ miles and has two bridges, Candy's Bridge and Folly's Footbridge (with stop gates). At the end, the canal takes a sudden turn left and a wall borders the towpath side. Just over the wall is the railway and, beyond that, some abandoned housing. In 1839, the Great Western Railway obtained an Act to build its new line along this narrow ridge and to divert the canal south. If you look over the wall, you can see where the canal once went and how the railway has stolen the route. During the diversion the canal was closed for 383 hours, for which the GWR paid the K&A £7,660 in compensation.

The canal now passes Darlington Wharf. In the 1830s passengers were able to take the 'Scotch' boat, a wrought-iron vessel brought from Scotland, from here to Bradford-on-Avon. There were two trips a day with forty passengers. It took an hour and a half and those on board were serenaded by a 'string band'. A little further on, the canal passes into the short (85 yd) Sydney Gardens Tunnel which goes under Beckford Road (A36) and into Sydney Gardens. When the canal was built, Sydney Gardens was privately owned and the proprietors demanded both 2,000 guineas and some landscaping work for the right to take the canal through their property. The canal was therefore hidden at both ends in tunnels and the section in between has two ornate wrought-iron bridges from George Stothert's foundry in Coalbrookdale. The second tunnel is of particular interest because it goes underneath Cleveland House which became the headquarters of the K&A Canal Company. As you go through, keep an eye open for a small shaft in the ceiling which goes up into the building. It's said that messages were put through from the office to passing boats via the shaft.

At the end of the tunnel, climb the steps on the right to cross the canal behind Cleveland House. The path turns right and continues down a slope to reach the left bank. Within a few hundred yards the canal passes Sydney Wharf, where the Somerset coal was unloaded. Go up a cobblestone path to the side of Sydney Wharf Road Bridge and then to Bathwick Road. Cross to the right-hand side of the bridge and go down some steps. Turn right to continue along the towpath to Bath Top Lock with its accompanying Stothert wrought-iron footbridge. This is the first lock since Bradford and the downstream end of the 'nine mile pound'. From here the canal makes a steep descent to the River Avon which is under ½ mile away.

The canal now descends quickly to Second Lock, after which it broadens to form a reservoir pound. The path curves round right past a solitary chimney on the other side of a hedge, to reach Abbey View Lock and Horseshoe Walk Bridge. The loss of water into the Avon was always a concern to the company and two pumping stations were built to take water back up the line. One pumping station was built at the bottom of the Widcombe flight and the other was just here. The lower engine pumped water into the pound above Abbey View Lock and the upper engine pushed it above Top Lock. Trouble arose when the company pumped water from the Bottom Lock chamber with the gate open, effectively removing water from the River Avon. The millowners didn't approve and took legal action to have it stopped. As a result, in 1855 the pumps were removed. All that remains of the upper station is the ornamental chimney that can be seen on the city side of the canal near Abbey View Lock.

Cross Horseshoe Walk and continue along the path. Wash House Lock is followed by another wrought-iron footbridge. Just before the church, the canal bends right to Bath Deep Lock, an amalgamation of two old locks to form the deepest lock in the entire British canal system at 18 ft 8 in (5.69 m). To save water, a pump moves water back upstream after use. To avoid crossing the busy Pulteney Road Bridge, cross the canal at the downstream lock gate. Steps go down to a concrete path which goes under the road. The path continues under a second road bridge (Baptist Chapel Bridge) and out to Thimble Mill Basin, a 'lagoon' in front of the Bath Hotel. The path soon

A group of children pose near Thimble Mill, Bath, in 1907
National Motor Museum

passes the final lock, Bottom or Widcombe Lock, which sits next to Thimble Mill, the lower of the two pump houses mentioned earlier. Go over Dolmeads Bridge to reach the western end of the 1810 K&A Canal and the River Avon, which appears massive in comparison.

From here both railway and bus stations can be reached by taking the higher of the two paths alongside the Avon. After 100 yd cross the green footbridge, Widcombe or Ha'penny Footbridge. To reach the station, walk on through a short tunnel. Turn left at the end for the BR station. The bus station is about 75 yd further on. If you prefer a prettier route, turn right at Dolmeads Bridge. The path soon reaches the famous Pulteney Bridge. Take the steps up to the road and turn left for the city centre.

Further Explorations

It's 92½ miles from the Thames at Reading to the centre of Bristol and, apart from the odd short stretch which can be readily got round, the whole length makes good, easy walking. It can be done either in one go as a week-long hike or as a series of day walks using public transport to get you back to the place where you started. The author's *Kennet & Avon Walk* (Cicerone Press) gives details of the route and the public transport available. The days can be organized as follows: Reading to Woolhampton; Woolhampton to Hungerford; Hungerford to Pewsey; Pewsey to Devizes; Devizes to Bradford-on-Avon; Bradford-on-Avon to Bath; and Bath to Bristol. It's a fine walk through great countryside and is recommended.

Those who believe a good walk is from their seat to the buffet car and back can also enjoy the eastern 40 miles of the K&A. BR's London to Westbury line runs parallel with the canal and affords views of such notable sights as the junction with the Thames, the Crofton pumping station, the western portal of the Savernake Tunnel, the locks at Monkey Marsh and Hungerford Marsh, and the Dun Aqueduct. True armchair canal-watching!

For those with more active feet, there are two walks which are clear 'musts'. The first is a walk of just over 3 miles up and down the Caen Hill flight of locks at Devizes. Towpathers should start at the Canal Trust Centre at Devizes Wharf (OS Landranger 173. OS ref: SU 004618). The wharf car park is well signposted from the through roads. The Trust Centre has a shop and museum, and there is a café nearby. From the centre, turn left and left again to reach Couch Lane and cross the canal at Cemetery Bridge. Turn left along the right-hand bank. This leads round to a lock and across Northgate Street. Pass three locks and the Black Horse pub before going through a small tunnel under Prison Bridge. Two locks further on is the Sir Hugh Stockwell Lock, otherwise known as Caen Hill Top Lock.

You are now at the summit of Caen Hill and have a fine view towards Melksham and Trowbridge. The hill is scaled by sixteen locks (Devizes has twenty-nine altogether in just 2¼ miles) which lift the canal 140 ft. Each lock is provided with its own reservoir, or side-pound, to provide additional water to prevent the draining of the system when in use. Each side-pound is about 6 ft deep and measures 70 yd by 45 yd. By walking down the towpath alongside the locks it is possible to realize the scale of the construction as well as the effort required by boatmen to pass up the flight. The best recorded time by a commercial boat was 2½ hours, although in a recent record attempt a crew scaled them in 2 hours 6 minutes. The locks were just about the last part of the K&A to be fully opened, both when the line was first built and when it was restored (in 1810 and 1990 respectively). During the course of the original construction, crews transhipped their goods onto a horse-drawn railway which ran beside the towpath.

Having reached the Lower Foxhangers Bridge at the bottom of the flight, it is possible to return by crossing at the bottom lock and walking on the opposite side of the side-pounds. You can't do this all the way and you will eventually come out at Queen's Lock, where there is a plinth commemorating the re-opening of the waterway in August 1990. From here it is a simple matter of retracing your steps back to Devizes Wharf.

Crofton is close to Great Bedwyn (OS Landranger 174. OS ref: SU 264624). You can park close to the well-signposted pumping station. Contained within a dull exterior are two beam engines built to pump water from Wilton Water reservoir to the K&A summit pound. The Boulton & Watt engine was installed in 1812 and is the oldest working beam engine in the world that is still doing its original job in its original position. The other engine was built in 1846 by Harvey's of Hayle in Cornwall. After falling into disrepair, the Canal Trust has restored both. The Boulton & Watt was resteamed for the first time, in the presence of Sir John Betjeman, in April 1970. On summer weekends one or other is in steam and open to the public. It's worth a visit, though check first for opening times with the Canal Trust at Devizes. Each engine can pump 11–12 tons of water per minute into a narrow leat which disappears off from the back of the building.

For a pleasant walk of about 3½ miles, leave the pumping station to go down some steps that pass under the railway and out to a lock (Crofton Bottom Lock). Cross the canal here and turn right. Over to the left is Wilton Water, the reservoir used by the pumping station. The walk gently bends right and passes a total of nine locks in 1½ miles. At the top lock you will be able to see the incoming water from the pumping station leat. The canal enters a deep cutting which eventually reaches Bruce or Savernake Tunnel. At 502 yd, the tunnel is the only major one on the K&A. There's no towpath and boats were pulled through by means of chains that hung from the walls. The horses, meanwhile, took a pleasant stroll up and over the hill.

For those with an OS map, it's possible to devise an alternative route back to Crofton. For those not in the mood for complex navigation, it's easier to turn round and gently amble back downhill to the pumping station.

Further Information

The canal you see today only exists because of the efforts of the K&A Canal Trust. It is well worth supporting.

Kennet & Avon Canal Trust Ltd,

Couch Lane,

Devizes,

Wiltshire SN10 1EB.

Tel: 0380-721279

This is also the number to call if you wish to know the opening times of the pumping stations.

The history of the K&A is related in:

Clew, K.R., *The Kennet & Avon Canal*, 3rd edition. David & Charles, 1985. I can heartily also recommend:

Quinlan, Ray, *The Kennet & Avon Walk. A walker's guide from London to Bristol*. Cicerone Press, 1991.

GEOProjects publishes a useful map of the entire canal. It is available locally or from: GEOProjects (UK) Ltd, Henley-on-Thames.

8
THE OXFORD CANAL
Tackley to Oxford

Introduction

The Oxford Canal is one of the oldest in the country. Surveyed by the doyen of canal engineers, James Brindley, the line has all the hallmarks of an early waterway as it meanders around the contours of the southern Midlands. Here is a canal that looks and feels much more like a river than a man-made waterway. It's rich in wildlife and justifiably popular. Perhaps its only drawback is the number of bodies that Inspector Morse seems to find in it!

The Oxford Canal starts at a junction with the Coventry Canal at Hawkesbury, 4 miles north of Coventry. From there the canal runs east via Ansty and Brinklow to the north of Rugby, before turning south to Braunston where the line meets the Grand Junction Canal. The main line of the Oxford now turns south-west to Napton where a second major junction, this time with the old Warwick & Napton Canal, offers a route to Birmingham and the West Midlands. The southern part of the Oxford then follows a convoluted line round Wormleighton, Claydon and Cropredy before reaching Banbury. The canal continues south by taking a more southerly line to Aynho, where the River Cherwell crosses the course of the canal in a kind of waterway crossroads. The line meanders past Upper and Lower Heyford and Enslow, where the River Cherwell and the canal merge for $1/2$ mile, only to separate at Shipton Weir Lock. The canal continues its journey through Thrupp and the outskirts of Kidlington before reaching Wolvercote, where the Duke's Cut takes a course west to the upper Thames. The main line then enters Oxford, where boaters can continue on to the Thames via Isis Lock.

Oxford, of course, is worth visiting even in the absence of a canal and the navigation is certainly not the reason why most people go there. But it offers a fascinating alternative to the almost over-visited Thames and the northern stretches of this walk make for as fine a stroll as you can find anywhere.

History

On 29 January 1768 an Act enabling the construction of the Coventry Canal from that city to the Trent & Mersey Canal at Fradley was passed by Parliament. This first step towards forming a navigable waterway between the Midlands and London having been made, the second, to take that line from Coventry to the Thames at Oxford, was sure to follow. Sir Roger Newdigate, MP for Oxford University, initiated that second step. At a meeting in Banbury on 13 April 1768, Newdigate, the Mayor of Banbury and others decided to ask James Brindley to survey a line from Coventry to Oxford. At a meeting in Banbury on 25 October, the scheme was received with great enthusiasm and funds in excess of £50,000 were promised. The bill proposed to Parliament on 29 November was widely supported. It was said that the canal would half the price of coal in Oxford and that the improved availability of roadstone would do wonders for turnpike maintenance. The main opposers were those associated with the Newcastle coal trade and a clause was inserted into the bill which prohibited movement of Warwickshire coal from the canal onto the southern Thames. With this amendment, the Act received Royal Assent on 21 April 1769.

Skinner's boats unloading at the old coal wharf in Oxford Canal Basin

British Waterways

The Act authorized a canal from Coventry to Oxford via Braunston, Napton and Banbury. Powers were obtained to raise £150,000 in £100 shares, with permission to obtain a further £50,000 should it be needed. Most of the money came from Oxford, although James Brindley himself is reported to have invested some £2,000. A maximum toll rate was set at 1/2d. per ton per mile. James Brindley was asked to make a more detailed survey with Samuel Simcock as his assistant. Brindley's plan (for what was later decided to be a canal of 7 ft width) was agreed at a meeting in the Three Tuns on 3 August 1769 and the first sod was cut at the junction with the Coventry Canal at Longford. This rather peculiar junction, which required the Coventry and the Oxford to run parallel for about a mile, was the result of some not atypical non-cooperation between the two companies. The more obvious junction at Hawkesbury was rejected by the Oxford when the Coventry demanded compensation for the loss of 2 miles worth of toll earnings if the proposed junction was moved. The wrangling over the siting of the junction meant that one was not actually forged until 1777. The present, more sensible and direct, junction at Hawkesbury was made in 1802.

By March 1771 the first 10 miles were built and the company was receiving toll revenue. When Brindley died in September 1772, Simcock took over as chief engineer and it was he who saw the line to completion. By 1774 40 miles were open to Napton, from where a busy coal trade to the towns to the south was started. This stretch included the 412 ft long Newbold Tunnel and a twelve-arch aqueduct at Brinklow (now an embankment). The year 1774 also saw improvements in the water supply to the summit pound between Napton and Claydon, with the incorporation of Boddington reservoir, the deepening of the summit pound and the construction of Clattercote reservoir near Banbury. In 1787 this was supplemented by another reservoir at Wormleighton. Funds were, however, already running low and completion to Banbury was only possible with the passage of a second Act on 20 March 1775, which enabled the raising of an additional £70,000. This allowed work to continue south so that by May 1776 the line reached Fenny Compton, where Simcock built a 1,138 yd long tunnel. Cropredy Wharf was opened on 1 October 1777 and on 30 March 1778 200 tons of coal arrived at Banbury, an event celebrated with great festivity. The canal was now 63³/₄ miles long and had cost £205,148. But by 1780 money was so short that all work on the line had stopped, a situation mirrored by the failure of the Coventry Canal Company to complete its line north to Fradley. Thus the two canals, although connected to each other, were still separated from the rest of the canal network and from the Thames. The Oxford was at least earning money. In the year ending August 1780 income was £6,982, although of this half went to pay loan interest.

The future of both canals was resolved by a meeting at Coleshill on

20 June 1782. It was agreed that the Oxford would complete its line to Oxford and that a combination of the Trent & Mersey and Birmingham & Fazeley companies would complete the Coventry to Fradley Junction. Despite these grand plans, the money was still wanting and it wasn't until September 1785 that the Oxford was in a position to ask Samuel Weston to make a survey of the River Cherwell from Banbury to Oxford. Although shown to be feasible, it was the original plan for a new cut that was incorporated in an Act passed on 11 April 1786 which enabled the raising of a further £60,000. This Act also removed the restriction on the movement of canal-borne coal along the Thames south of Oxford. Robert Whitworth was asked to resurvey the Banbury to Oxford section and James Barnes was appointed as resident engineer for this last phase.

On 30 August 1787 the canal was open to Northbrook, just north of Tackley, and by January 1789 Samuel Simcock was preparing plans for the canal's terminus near Hythe Bridge in Oxford. The entire works reached a conclusion on 1 January 1790 when a fleet of boats entered Oxford and the band of the Oxford Militia played suitably celebratory numbers. The canal as built was 91 miles long and had cost approximately £307,000. In addition to the wharves in central Oxford, by 1796 boats were also able to navigate onto the Thames via Duke's Cut, a channel which left the canal near Wolvercote and entered the Thames near King's Weir. This had been built by the company following a suggestion from the Duke of Marlborough who

A picture taken by E. Temple Thurston during his trip along the Oxford Canal in 1910 or 1911. This picture was taken at Cropredy Lock and is thought to show his boatman, Eynsham Harry, on the right
Temple Thurston Archive, The Boat Museum Archive

owned the land. This route to the northern Thames was later supplemented by one to the southern, with the opening of Isis Lock in 1796.

With the completion of the Birmingham & Fazeley Canal and the Coventry as far as Fazeley, a line to Birmingham and the Potteries was now open and trade improved significantly. There were some initial problems with water supply but these were solved by the installation of steam engines to back pump water up to the summit pound. This shortage of water delayed the payment of any dividends during the early years. However, by 1795 a half-yearly dividend of 2 per cent was paid and it wasn't too long before the company was in a position to be much more rewarding to its investors. At this time coal was the major cargo to be carried along the canal. In the year ending 1792–3, 55,893 tons of coal were shipped from Coventry, of which 9,787 tons were brought into Oxford. In addition to this, coal from Wyken and Hawkesbury would also have been moved. In 1795 the Oxford company purchased its own coal wharf in Reading and later acquired wharves at Wallingford and Abingdon. The preponderance of coal as a cargo suggests that many boats must have made the return journey empty.

Although the Oxford Canal had significantly reduced the navigable distance from the Midlands (London to Birmingham via the Thames & Severn Canal was 269$^{1}/_{2}$ miles, compared with 227 via the Oxford), in 1791 the

Isis Lock and Bridge near central Oxford

route was still considered to be indirect and slow. In particular the Thames was difficult and often impassable. A new proposal for two Warwick Canals and the Grand Junction Canal in 1791 meant that the distance between London and Birmingham could soon be reduced to just 137 miles of modern, fast waterway. The Oxford's response to the threat was immediate. A proposal for the Hampton Gay, or London & Western Canal was published in direct competition to the GJC. The L&W was to run from Shipton-under-Cherwell via Thame, Wendover and Amersham to Isleworth. Although still 30 miles longer than the GJC, it offered a much more direct, Thames-free, line to London compared with the route along the southern Oxford. For a while it looked possible that both might be built. However, the political clout of the GJC meant that parliamentary interest concentrated on the GJC and the L&W eventually evaporated in return for the GJC guaranteeing the Oxford minimum receipts of £10,000 p.a., a guarantee which in fact was never called on. The two Warwick Canals, the Warwick & Birmingham and the Warwick & Napton, were open in 1800 and the GJC was opened to London in 1805. Traffic from Birmingham to London now passed along the Warwick Canals to Napton and then took the Oxford for 5 miles to Braunston, where it entered the GJC. The traffic along the 5 mile Napton to Braunston section was to become 'a nice little earner' for the Oxford company.

By 1801 the Oxford's receipts reached £37,996 and it was able to pay an 8 per cent dividend. Just eight years later these figures had risen to £79,438 and 25 per cent. About two-fifths of the traffic along the canal was coal shipped primarily from Wednesbury and Warwickshire. Other goods included limestone, roadstone, iron, salt and general merchandise. The canal was in all respects a success. By 1832 the use of the canal was such that yet more water was needed and the Boddington reservoir was enlarged. But perhaps the most important development was the modernization of the northern canal. The stimulus to update the line was the announcement in November 1827 of the London & Birmingham Junction Canal that would have run directly from the Stratford-upon-Avon Canal at Earlswood to the GJC at Braunston, thereby bypassing the Oxford completely. Although the L&BJ was never built, the Oxford went ahead with improvements which shortened it by 13⅝ miles, mostly by making direct cuts where Brindley had woven great loops. The work included a rebuilding of the junction at Braunston and a new, shorter Newbold Tunnel. Charles Vignole was employed as engineer. The work was enabled by an Act of 1829 and completed by May 1834 at a cost of £167,172.

The canal company entered the 1840s in a healthy position. Receipts in 1842 totalled £73,119 and a dividend of 30 per cent was issued. In that year 20,859 boats had passed through the Hillmorton Locks and 9,900 had passed through the summit pound at Claydon. By 1848 the company was able to pay off its debt. The canal had developed a fearful reputation for exploiting its position as the linking canal between the Midlands and the GJC, and for overcharging. Several meetings were held during the 1840s at which the other companies involved in the north–south route met with a view to increasing business. On each occasion the Oxford were accused of pursuing a policy which enabled the company to pay a 30 per cent dividend, whereas the other companies were only able to muster 7 per cent. In 1845 the position was such that the GJC and the Warwick Canals threatened to amalgamate and thus isolate the Oxford entirely. This finally sparked the Oxford into action. It promptly agreed to cooperate with its neighbours and to reduce tolls along its part of the line. But by that time, the effects of the railway were already being felt.

In 1826 a plan for a railway to run from London to Birmingham by way of Oxford and Banbury was published. This scheme came to nought but the London & Birmingham Railway, which almost directly followed the course of the GJC, opened in 1838. Even though this line was some considerable distance to the east, it immediately had an effect on trade along the Oxford. Toll receipts at Braunston were almost halved in just three years. Conversely, the opening of the Great Western Railway line from Didcot to Oxford in 1844 had a positive affect on the fortunes of the southern part of the Oxford, with a minor increase in toll receipts. It was not until 1850 that a GWR subsidiary continued the route north through Enslow, Aynho and Heyford to Banbury. The next phase, completed in 1853, took the line on to Warwick and thus to Birmingham. Also in 1850, the Buckinghamshire Railway was opened from Banbury to join the London & Birmingham. The same company then opened a branch via Bicester to Oxford. The competition for coal delivery was now intense and the Oxford was forced to reduce its toll rates to Banbury by 80 per cent. This maintained the tonnage carried along the canal but seriously reduced receipts. In 1848 420,000 tons of cargo were carried with receipts of £56,000. In 1858 the figures were 400,000 tons and £24,700. As a consequence the 1858 dividend was down to 8¼ per cent. By the 1860s, traffic along the southern line to Cropredy, Aynho and Oxford itself had fallen heavily.

Despite the difficulties, the Oxford remained fiercely independent and managed to maintain the amount of cargo carried to the end of the century. Indeed, at the beginning of the twentieth century, there were even suggestions that a new modernization programme be implemented as a way of once again competing with the railways. Needless to say, nothing came of any of these plans and the First World War saw the beginning of the end of the Oxford as a commercial waterway. However, in 1919 286,459 tons of cargo were still being carried and the company implemented a post-war maintenance and improvement programme. In the 1930s the new Grand Union Canal Company made an attempt to increase traffic on its London to

Birmingham route. As part of this it agreed to undertake work on the Napton to Braunston section of the Oxford. It improved the banking and rebuilt two bridges so that 12 ft 6 in wide barges could navigate between the old GJC and the old Warwick & Napton Canal. Included in this deal, the Grand Union guaranteed the Oxford minimum toll receipts for this section of its line. By the time of the Second World War the Oxford was still able to deliver an 8 per cent dividend. Coal still formed the bulk of the cargo carried. A wartime government report recognized the line's strategic importance and recommended that it be fully maintained just in case the GJC was blocked. But after the war the line declined considerably. The situation was not improved by nationalization in 1948. The canal now began to lose money and the Board of Survey classified the northern section of the canal as 'to be retained' and the southern section under 'waterways having insufficient commercial prospects to justify their retention'. Such was the concern that the Inland Waterways Association held its 1955 rally at Banbury with a view to promoting the Oxford as worthy of retention. The popular cause was justly supported and by 1968 the future of the southern section was recovered. The Transport Act listed the Oxford, all of it, as a cruiseway and thus gave British Waterways the remit to maintain the line to the required standard. Today the Oxford is one of the best-loved holiday waterways.

The Walk

Start:	Tackley BR station (OS ref: SP 484206)
Finish:	Oxford near BR station (OS ref: SP 508064)
Distance:	11¼ miles/18 km
Map:	OS Landranger 164 (Oxford)
Outward:	BR Oxford to Tackley (enquiries: 0734-595911)
Car park:	Oxford has numerous car parks but try one of the well-signposted park and rides
Public transport:	Trains from London and Didcot going north call at Oxford

This walk can be shortened to 2½ miles each way by parking near the canal at Enslow (OS ref: SP 479183), just off the Oxford to Banbury A423, and walking south to the Boat Inn at Thrupp (OS ref: SP 480157). This option would take in some of the most pleasant and interesting parts of the full walk. There is room for on-road parking at Thrupp for those lucky enough to have like-minded friends. Otherwise, lunch at the Boat should be succour enough for the return stroll.

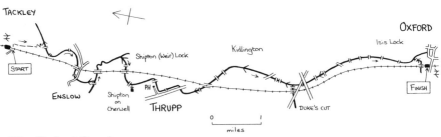

The Oxford Canal

From Tackley station, cross the railway via two pedestrian gates at the Oxford end of the platform. Follow the dirt road right and on for 1/2 mile to a T-junction. Turn left and after 200 yd bear right with the track. Go over a bridge which crosses one stream of the River Cherwell and on along a fenced path. This winds over a weir and round the perimeter of Flights Mill to reach the canal at Pigeons (or Pidgeons) Lock. Bear left down the side of the bridge and turn right to start the walk along the right-hand bank.

When I was here, the canal was blanketed with inch-thick sheets of ice. One intrepid boater had broken through to leave a series of mini-icebergs in his wake. The resultant aftermath produced a gentle Swiss cowbell-like tinkling sound which eerily reverberated around the freezing fog. There was a gorgeous, early morning tranquillity which was only disturbed by me stomping my feet to get warm. Unable to partake of the pub that formerly stood here at Pigeon's Lock, I put on my gloves and made off to go under bridge 214 and on to lifting bridge 215, Caravan Lift Bridge. The lifting bridge is one of those wonderfully simple inventions that make certain aspects of eighteenth-century engineering so enjoyable. The type found on the Oxford Canal (there were thirty-eight of them originally) was designed by James Brindley. The platform is counterbalanced by projecting beams which, when the bridge is open, lie horizontally and, when closed, rise accordingly. The water channel narrows to just 7 ft, i.e. narrow boat width, at the bridge to reduce the weight and cost. The whole thing, made mostly of wood, seems wholly in keeping with the pleasant pastoral nature of the canal; a highly functional object beautifully designed.

The canal swings round to join the River Cherwell to the right and you should continue along a narrow isthmus before going under the railway for the first time. The village to the left is Enslow, an important point on the canal as it is on the road which joins the villages of Islip and Woodstock. In the early days there was a flourishing coal trade from Enslow Bridge Wharf, a business that continued until after the Second World War. In the early twentieth century, the wharf also became an important canal/railway transfer point for cement brought along the canal from the works at Kirtlington, just north of Pigeons Lock. The narrowing of the waterway near the wharf suggests the position of a gauging point where tolls were applied.

The walk passes the old Enslow Bridge (from where if you cross you can reach the Rock of Gibraltar pub, formerly the wharfinger's house) and, after going over a stile, under the new road bridge. The inherently meandering nature of this, one of our earliest canals, can be seen as, once more, the line of the waterway swings east. Had the Oxford been built fifty years later by Thomas Telford we would perhaps be on a walk that would have been, say, 2 miles shorter. Brindley, however, did not have the technology to build the dramatic cuttings or embankments that embellish Telford's Birmingham & Liverpool Junction Canal. Brindley built his waterways to meander around the contours, following the easiest line. The Oxford is thus very much an example of an early canal which was later to be considered somewhat out of date and slow to use. Improvements in the nineteenth century meant that many of the meanders were bypassed with newer straight cuts. Some of the former can still be traced (see Further Explorations).

Heading south the canal comes, after Baker's Lock, to physically join the River Cherwell just south of Enslow. The Cherwell was made navigable from Oxford to Banbury, probably under the direction of Andrew Yarranton, in the late seventeenth century. It was still navigable here in 1777 and formed the natural route for this stretch of the canal. The towpath crosses the river by an iron bridge built in 1909. It is a splendid spot and remarkably remote. Kingfishers and herons abound and, even at midday, a tawny owl called from the small copse across the channel. A little further on along the combined waterway, there is a post with DIS written on it beside the towpath. You will see others along the way. As part of the company's by-laws boats within 200 yd of a lock with the water level in their favour had the right of way. The DIS post was positioned so that there was no dispute as to who was first to be within the required distance.

After going under the railway, the combined river/canal goes through a series of sharp turns through fine open countryside, only to separate again at Shipton (Weir) Lock. Here you turn right while the river goes straight on through weirs near the village of Hampton Gay. Shipton Lock has a fall of just 2^1/$_2$ ft and if a standard narrow lock had been built here it would not have passed sufficient water down the line to supply the next lock (Roundham) which was of more normal depth. Indeed, it may have acted more like a dam. So the lock chamber at Shipton was built in a hexagonal shape, which permits a much greater flow of water. A similar lock was built for similar reasons where the Cherwell and the canal cross at Aynho, just south of Banbury. According to a photograph in Hugh Compton's book, there was formerly a small lock-keeper's cottage to the right of the lock. Cross the canal via the bridge at the downstream end to take up the left-hand bank. The towpath passes a lift bridge to reach a rail bridge and the abutments of a former rail bridge. On Christmas Eve 1874, a train jumped the rails just here and crashed onto the frozen canal. Some thirty-four people died, many of whom are buried in nearby Hampton Gay churchyard.

After passing a single-gate stop lock and going under Shipton Bridge (no. 220), you arrive at Shipton-on-Cherwell with its loftily positioned church that stares down on passing boaters and towpathers. Anyone who has read Temple Thurston's *The Flower of Gloster* will recognize Shipton as the place where the traveller spent his first night on board boat. Here the author pondered the passage of time and professed an interest in having his bones laid to rest amid the green grass of the churchyard.

For a while the Cherwell runs alongside the canal but then the 'cut' broadens and turns abruptly right. This is Thrupp and the site of a BW maintenance yard. Cross the lift bridge (Aubrey's Lift Bridge) and continue past the houses and cottages along the right-hand bank. At the end of the village, the path passes The Boat, as fine a place to have lunch as any to be found. TV fans may recall that this is where Inspector Morse and Sergeant Lewis (sorry, I mean John Thaw and Kevin Whately) went to find breakfast after starting their investigation in Colin Dexter's *Riddle of the Third Mile*. The mutilated corpse had been found in the canal here at Thrupp by some passing holiday boaters. Nasty.

The canal soon bends left and passes another pub, the Jolly Boatman, before going under Sparrowgap Bridge and running alongside the busy A423 into Kidlington. Before entering town, the canal again bends sharply right to go under Langford Lane Bridge and into an industrial area of north Kidlington. Roundham Lock and Bridge are soon followed by a railway bridge. The quiet suburbs of Kidlington now dominate the left bank. Go under two more bridges (Bullers and Yarnton) and pass another lock (Kidlington Green Lock) before re-emerging into open country. Originally the canal wasn't coming this way at all but was going to run about a mile to the west through Begbroke and Yarnton. Samuel Simcock changed Brindley's planned route in January 1788.

The canal continues under a pipe bridge and the Woodstock Road (Kings) Bridge, while the ears are pummelled by the noise from the new A34 road way over to the left. The towpath passes a peculiarly positioned pillbox to reach Duke's Lock. Here there is a lengthsman's cottage and a roving bridge which passes over the entrance to Duke's Cut. This narrow channel, which runs to the Thames near King's Lock and Weir, was dug in 1789 at the request of the 4th Duke of Marlborough to link up with his Wolvercote paper mill. The mill is actually on a stream which runs parallel with the canal about 1/2 mile to the west. Until 1796 the cut was the only link between Oxford and the Thames. The cut enabled Warwickshire coal to be brought to the mill via the canal. The lock at the entrance is effectively a stop lock. The level of the canal is normally higher than the river but in flood the river may be 2 ft higher than the canal. Morse fans will of course recognize Duke's Cut as the site of yet more foul deeds. In *The Wench is Dead* Colin Dexter asks the inspector to investigate a murder which occurred in 1859. This, of course, he does with his usual seemingly somnolent style. Continue walking along the main canal to go under the substantial Oxford–Witney A40 road bridge that was built in 1933. A short distance further on is one of those peculiar juxtapositions that occur periodically along our waterways: an almost delicate and appealing eighteenth-century lift bridge and an elephantine and bullying twentieth-century dual carriageway road bridge.

You are now approaching the outskirts of north Oxford as you pass Perry's Lift Bridge and Wolvercote Lock. From here almost into central Oxford, the canalside is littered with a succession of houseboats. The next mile takes in a road bridge, Ball's Bridge, the last railway bridge and St Edward's Lift Bridge before reaching a factory which dominates the left-hand bank. Here bridge 239A is a lift bridge of a more modern kind, electrically powered and an important route from one part of the works to the other. There is now just over a mile into central Oxford and the factory gives way to suburban housing with gardens running down to the canal. Temple Thurston suggested that the building of these houses was like the growth 'of some unsightly fungus' nurtured by 'jerry-builders – men of execrable taste, whose only thought is to build for profit'. As he then goes on to say that they wouldn't last, he may well be surprised to see them still here and quite well thought of compared with what has come since.

After Frenchhay Lift Bridge the canal goes on to Aristotle Bridge, from where there is access to shops to the left. Bridge 242 is followed by a works bridge that runs from a metal castings works known as Lucy's Foundry, which has its own wharf and canalside loading area. The stroll through the suburb of Jericho is a popular spot for dog-walkers and joggers and leads to the fine cast-iron bridge that goes over the head of Isis Lock. The waterway to the right is the River Isis, a tributary of the Thames, the main channel of which is just a few hundred yards to the right. Boaters heading towards the river pass through the lock and turn right to go under the railway and out, along a channel called the Sheepwash, to the river. Although the canal was fully opened in 1790, the Isis Lock connection with the Thames wasn't built until 1796. It's construction allowed boats to avoid a convoluted section of the Thames west of Wolvercote.

Cross the bridge and walk on with the canal left and Isis right. The canal ends at Hythe Bridge, while the river continues south to enter the Thames. From 1839 there was a floating chapel moored on the river just before the bridge, positioned to enhance the moral and spiritual well-being of the boat people. In 1868 the vessel sank and a new on-shore chapel was built in Hythe Bridge Street. Originally the canal also continued under the road bridge and on to two wharves. If you go up to the road and peer over the wall, the site of Worcester Street Wharf can be seen. It is now a car park. The line of the canal bent left so that it continued across the open space and under Worcester Street to end at the New Road Wharf. The bridges here were built to barge width so that boats from the Thames could use the wharves as well as the narrow boats that had ventured along the canal. Interestingly, however, as a protectionist measure the Oxford company always steadfastly refused permission for the landing of coal from the Thames at either of its city centre wharves. Both wharves were infilled after the Second World War, although the land was actually sold to Lord Nuffield (William Morris) in 1936. Nuffield College now sits atop New Road Wharf.

Oxford town centre and the bus station can be reached by turning left along Hythe Bridge Street. The railway station is reached by turning right.

Further Explorations

Sadly, many sections of the Oxford's towpath are either in a very poor state or even non-existent, a problem that arose from the destructive wash of motorized vessels. This is a pity because it would undoubtedly make for fine walking all the way along. This should not deter the hardy towpather, who can savour the Oxford's delights with a series of short walks.

A walk of 7^1/$_2$ miles starts at Napton on the Hill (OS Landranger 151. OS ref: SP 464611). The village can be found to the south of the Leamington Spa to Daventry A425. Buses run twice daily from Leamington (G & G Travel enquiries: 0926-885555). For those with cars, park in the centre of the village near the Crown pub. To start the walk turn right from the pub past the small general stores and telephone box. The road bends right along New Street past the post office and Napton Christadelphian Meeting Room. It then turns left to form Thornton Lane and then Chapel Green. As the main road bends right again, go straight on along a much smaller lane which is signposted to Marston Doles. This pleasant country lane runs for just over a mile. Halfway along, those with keen eyes may spot a rundown building in a field to the right. This is the engine house that will be discussed later. At a T-junction turn right to reach a bridge over the canal. Cross and turn left through the gate to reach Napton Top Lock. Here turn left to take up the left-hand bank of the canal.

At Napton Top Lock the canal reaches its summit pound. The next lock south is at Claydon, 5 miles as the crow flies, 11 as the narrow boat meanders. The route, of course, goes north past a second lock before taking the first of the giant bends that mark Brindley's canal-building style. Within a mile is the Engine House arm, a narrow strip of water that leaves from the right-hand bank. This channel was built so that boats could take coal to a steam engine which pumped water up the canal from below Napton Bottom Lock into the summit pound. As you may have seen, the engine house is derelict and the job is apparently now carried out by electric motors.

The walk continues past six locks with fine views to Napton windmill before reaching Napton Bottom Lock. The canal now bends sharply left to go around Napton Hill with its massive quarry scar. Continue past a boat-yard and on to a main road bridge and the Napton Bridge Inn. Continue to the next two bridges and Napton Narrowboats yard. You will return to Napton by turning right at the second bridge. However, keen towpathers will want to walk briefly on past the boat-yard to see Napton Junction. Here the Warwick & Napton Canal (now the Grand Union) takes a line, left, to Warwick and then to central Birmingham. The Oxford, meanwhile, carries on to Braunston where it forms a junction with the Grand Junction Canal for London. Return to the bridge and turn left. Go over the crossroads and up the road which winds round some houses into central Napton and the Crown Inn.

For those who prefer their walks to be around a mile in length and to involve a pub, there are two offerings. Between Banbury and Southam, the A423 goes over the Oxford Canal near Fenny Compton. If you park near the road bridge at SP 436523 (Landranger 151), you can look down to the canal as it passes through a cutting. This part of the Oxford is known as the 'tunnel'. This is because when the canal was first opened here in 1778 a 1,138 yd long tunnel was built to take the line through the hill. The problem was that it was just 12 ft high and 9 ft wide and was responsible for endless traffic jams. In 1840 the land above the tunnel was purchased from Christ Church, Oxford and a central passing place opened up with two tunnels either side. In 1870 these were removed and hence the whole tunnel opened out into a cutting. On one side of the road bridge there is a fine cast-iron footbridge dating from the first 'opening out', which takes the towpath from the southern to the northern bank. A well-trodden path leaves the left-hand side of the road bridge on the other side of the road to go down to the canal. Once on the path turn right, cross the footbridge and walk along the left-hand bank, past Cowroast boat-yard and on to the George & Dragon pub at Fenny Compton Wharf, a total distance of just under a mile. The best option for returning is back along the canal.

In the 1820s the Oxford company was aware that the canal was showing its age. It was both slow to use and often highly tortuous as it relentlessly followed the contours around the countryside. As a consequence it set about a programme of improvements which took 14 miles off the 43 miles of canal between Hawkesbury and Napton. At Newbold-on-Avon (Landranger 140. OS ref: SP 487773) the former circuitous route of 1¼ miles was shortened

The entrance to the old canal tunnel and St Botolph's Church at Newbold-on-Avon

to just 1/2 mile by the straightening of the line and the construction of a new tunnel. From the B4112 at Newbold, go along a narrow lane at the back of the Boat Inn and past the Barley Mow to reach the towpath of the northern Oxford. If you turn left you can follow the curve of the canal round to the new Newbold Tunnel. It was built in 1834 as part of the improvement programme and is 350 yd long. It's a typical late canal tunnel: it has a towpath on either side and is wide enough for narrow boats to pass each other. If you continue onwards to the next road bridge, the original line of the canal can be seen on what appears to be a junction. The canal went left here and across the fields before swinging back into Newbold. To see the old tunnel, return to the Boat Inn and turn right to reach St Botolph's churchyard. Go through the gate and bear right past the church to a stile. Here is the old canal bed and, to the right, the red-brick entrance of the original 125 yd long Newbold Tunnel. It is considerably narrower than the new tunnel and does not have a towpath. The tunnel runs under the churchyard and the road to come out along the lane in front of the two pubs to join the present route. Surprisingly, the tunnel (although not the land above it) was still owned by British Waterways as recently as March 1991, when it was auctioned for £1,000 for Comic Relief.

Further Information

There is no Oxford Canal society as such. However, within the Inland Waterways Association, there is an Oxford branch. To find out about meetings first contact IWA head office, the telephone number and address of which can be found in Appendix B.

For more detail on the history of the canal, the best available source is:

Compton, H.J., *The Oxford Canal*. David & Charles, 1976.

Those who wish to read of the more seamy side of life on the Oxford Canal should head for:

Dexter, Colin, *The Riddle of the Third Mile*. Pan Books, 1983.

Dexter, Colin, *The Wench is Dead*. Pan Books, 1989.

9
THE REGENT'S CANAL
Camden Town to Paddington

Introduction

In the midst of the hustle and bustle of the nation's capital exists the most pleasant of watery retreats. The Regent's Canal has that peculiarly rural feel that it shares with the city's great parks. It's an urbanized pastoral haven, a rustic metropolis. Whatever it is, it's a lifeline. Not that it has always been fully appreciated. It was once viewed solely as a convenient repository, a place for everything that was no longer worth anything. Luckily, the councils, amenity groups and British Waterways have removed the junk that once encrusted the canal and the line is now a popular spot for joggers, lunching office workers, the inevitable fishermen and, of course, the ever-swarming towpathers.

The Regent's Canal leaves the old Grand Junction Canal at Little Venice, a lagoon a few hundred yards north of Paddington station. After $1/2$ mile the line enters Maida Hill Tunnel which goes under the Edgware Road to reappear near Lisson Grove and Lord's cricket ground. After a further $1/2$ mile the canal reaches the northern perimeter of Regent's Park. Here the waterway curves around the outskirts of the park and through London Zoo to arrive at Cumberland Basin where it turns abruptly left. After passing Camden Lock and Hampstead Road, the line enters Kentish Town and St Pancras. It then continues under the Caledonian Road to enter Islington Tunnel and comes out near the Angel tube station and the City Road. The canal now enters the heart of London's East End, through Hackney and Bethnal Green to reach Victoria Park, where the Hertford Union Canal runs east to join the Lee Navigation. It is now just $11/2$ miles through Mile End and Stepney to the Limehouse Basin and the River Thames.

Walking through cities isn't everybody's idea of a good day out but this short stroll has bags of interest and many surprises, not the least of which is the friendliness of the locals who, of those I met, seem to have a genuine interest in their canal. One to do instead of the Christmas shopping.

History

There was no doubt that by the end of the eighteenth century, London was still relatively isolated from the rapidly industrializing midland and northern towns. The need to improve the transport of coal and goods to and from the capital was becoming a major concern, remedied initially in 1790 when the Oxford Canal opened up the route from the Midlands via the Thames, and on 10 July 1801 when the Grand Junction Canal was opened to Paddington, a spot at one end of the 'New Road' which then formed the northern boundary of the city. From Paddington cargo was transhipped onto carts for haulage into the centre of town. It wasn't too long after the opening of Paddington Basin that it was suggested that a new canal be built to run parallel with the New Road from Paddington to the city and then the Thames near the expanding London Docks. The advantage of not having to tranship goods from canal onto cart was widely agreed. In July 1802 a line for the London Canal was surveyed from Paddington Basin to the New River (Islington), the Commercial Road and the Thames. Subscriptions of £400,000 were quickly raised by a committee headed by Sir Christopher Baynes, but with the protestations of local landowners and the refusal of the GJC to provide a water supply, the scheme was dropped.

By 1810 the idea was once again in circulation. The key protagonist at this time was a former committee member of the Coventry Canal and one-time canal boat owner, Thomas Homer, who suggested a line running parallel to the New Road from Paddington through Islington to the Thames at Limehouse where he planned to build a ship dock. John Rennie reported favourably on the scheme and Homer sought to enthuse the influential. At about the same time, the architect John Nash had been appointed to develop the Marylebone Park Estate, later to be renamed Regent's Park, for the Commissioners for Woods and Forests. Homer saw advantages in linking the canal with the estate and invited Nash to take responsibility for the canal. Nash was seemingly delighted with the idea of boats sailing gracefully through the park and accepted. Nash and his assistant, James Morgan, were joined by an engineer, James Tate, to examine Homer's proposed route and with minor adjustments agreed it. Within the park, the canal was to be combined with a broad ornamental lake which was to be a central feature. By August 1811 this link with the new Regent's Park was such that the canal was renamed the Prince Regent's Canal. In a prospectus the cost of the new navigation was estimated at £280,000.

By the time a bill was presented to parliament in the summer of 1812, Nash had changed his mind about having a commercial canal running through his new up-market gardens. As a result, the route was pushed out to the northern edge of the park, the banks were to be built up to nearly 25 ft to conceal the line and the towing path was moved to the northern side. With this change, and despite the protestations of the Paddington wharfingers who feared loss of trade, the bill received Royal Assent on 13 July 1812, granting powers to build the canal and to raise the necessary £400,000.

The canal proprietors met for the first time on 10 August 1812 at the Freemason's Tavern at St Giles-in-the-Fields. Charles Munro was made chairman, John Nash was appointed as a director and John Morgan as engineer, architect and land surveyor. Thomas Homer, who had started the whole scheme, was appointed superintendent. Morgan estimated that the line would cost £299,729 to build and the go-ahead to start the construction work was given. Curiously, none of these individuals had experience of canal building and the committee was forced to offer the design of much of the line, such as tunnels and locks, out to competition. This proved to be a fruitless exercise, with none of the entrants' designs being accepted by the committee. In the end, Morgan was instructed to draw up his own designs.

The construction work started on 14 October 1812, with James Tate as contractor. Interestingly, the Act demanded that the part of the canal that passed through Regent's Park should be finished within twelve months. This they just failed to do as it was completed by 11 November 1813. The stretch between Little Venice and Hampstead Road, with the exception of Maida Hill Tunnel, was finished six months later. The 2¹/₂ mile lock-free stretch between the GJC at Little Venice to Hampstead Road was officially opened on the Prince Regent's birthday, 12 August 1816.

On 4 April 1815 it was discovered that Thomas Homer had sequestered some of the company's funds, a charge he admitted before fleeing the country. He was later arrested and sentenced to transportation. The funds were never recovered and shareholders had to make up the missing amount. Financial problems also threatened the completion of the rest of the canal, with work being suspended for a while. Although £400,000 had been authorized, the company had only been able to raise £254,100. An Act in 1816, designed to produce a further £200,000, was passed but still the necessary monies were slow in coming. The problem was resolved through the receipt of funds from the Commissioners for the Issue of Exchequer Bills, a kind of early job creation scheme set up by the Poor Employment Act of 1817. Following a survey of the line by Thomas Telford, the commissioners agreed to loan the company £200,000 if it could raise £100,000 of its own. With the confidence of the investors thus restored, the extra funds were raised relatively easily. By the end of 1818 the Islington Tunnel was finished and it was firmly hoped that the line would be open by the end of 1819. In fact the end of 1819 saw the raising of another £105,000. This extra delay meant that it wasn't until 1 August 1820 that the Regent's Canal was officially opened from the Grand Junction Canal at Paddington through to the Thames at Limehouse. A flag-covered barge full of proprietors, including the Earl of Macclesfield, the company chairman, set off from Maiden Lane (now York Way, King's Cross) followed by two military bands playing 'enlivening airs'. The completed canal is 8¹/₂ miles long and drops 86 ft through twelve broad locks from Little Venice to Limehouse. There are thirty-six road bridges, nine footbridges, ten railway bridges and two tunnels. The new line had cost £710,000.

In its first year after opening, the company reported the carriage of nearly 195,000 tons of cargo and this steadily increased. In the year ending April 1829, it carried over 488,721 tons and in 1834–5 this had risen to 624,827, earning some £28,930 in tolls. The company was able to clear its debt to the commissioners of £235,000 in 1828 and the first dividend of 12s. 6d. per £100 share was paid in 1830. Contrary to expectations, nearly three-quarters of the traffic using the line came from the Thames Dock rather than from the inland GJC. The trade was primarily in coal, timber, road materials, bricks, lime and sand. The success of the line encouraged Sir George Duckett to build his Hertford Union Canal, which joined the Regent's with the Lee Navigation in 1830. However, the link line was never a great success, even after it was rendered toll-free for a period in 1831. In

The Great Northern Railway's interchange depot near St Pancras Lock on the Regent's Canal

British Waterways

1848 the line was blocked off to avoid water loss and in 1857 it was finally purchased by the Regent's Canal Company.

It was just seventeen years after the opening of the canal that the first railway from the Midlands reached London. Stephenson's London & Birmingham Railway of 1837 followed roughly the same route as the GJC and immediately took traffic from it. In 1852 the London & York railway was opened to a temporary terminus in Maiden Lane, or York Road as it became, and the Midland Railway reached London in 1868. The position of the Regent's, running from Paddington Basin across the lines of all the northern railway termini to the Thames, attracted considerable interest from those who saw an opportunity to convert it to a railway line. The first offer from a company so interested arrived in September 1845. In the same year the company's own engineer, William Radford, suggested that it make the conversion itself. The initial reluctance of the committee was overcome when an outside consortium offered to buy the line for a million pounds. However, the scheme for what was intended to be the Regent's Canal Railway floundered as the consortium failed to raise the necessary funds. Several other attempts to make the conversion were made but none of them was able to generate any financial enthusiasm, or, as in the case of the Central London Railway & Dock Co., were defeated in Parliament following opposition from, among others, the GJC. By this time the canal was a highly profitable concern. In 1876–7 trade along the line was some 1,427,047 tons p.a., with receipts of £92,877 and profits of £46,559. A large proportion of this income was derived from warehouse and port dues. It wasn't until 31 March 1883, when the canal was taken over by The Regent's Canal City Docks Railway Company for £1,170,585, that a conversion plan looked like becoming a reality. But even though the company changed its name in 1892 to the North Metropolitan Railway and Canal Co., the necessary capital of £2,500,000 wasn't forthcoming. By 1904 defeat was admitted when the name reverted to the Regent's Canal and Dock Company.

In 1905 the Regent's Canal carried 1,045,184 tons of cargo and had receipts of £92,000. The main business at the time was the shipment of coal to local gasworks. Despite this, more and more traffic was being lost to the railways and then to the roads. Unusually for canal companies, the response of the GJC and the Regent's was to enter into a period of collaboration. In 1914 the two companies formed a joint committee of directors. After the First World War the companies decided to merge. To do this the Regent's bought the GJC (which already owned the Old Union and Old Grand Union canals in Leicestershire and the three Warwick canals (the Warwick & Birmingham, the Warwick & Napton and the Birmingham & Warwick Junction to form the Grand Union Canal Company. This was achieved on 1 January 1929 at a cost of £801,442 for the GJC and £136,003 for the Warwick canals. The grouping was expanded in January 1932 when the

Grand Union purchased the Leicester and Loughborough Navigations and the Erewash Canal for a total of £75,423. For the first time, the inland waterway route from London to Birmingham and London to the Trent was under one roof.

The new Grand Union was committed to expanding the use of the line. The key parts of its plan involved making the canal to Birmingham suitable for barges and providing an improved design of barge to work it. The improvement budget for 1931 amounted to one million pounds (with the help of a government guarantee) and a new class of boat, the Royalty Class, of 12 ft 6 in beam, was in production. The company also started its own carrying company by buying Associated Canal Carriers Ltd, renaming it the Grand Union Canal Carrying Co. Ltd.

The history of the company after this period of hopeful expansion is one of disappointment. No dividends were paid on ordinary shares between 1933 and 1945, and in 1948 it was nationalized and put under the control of the British Transport Commission (later the British Waterways Board). The Regent's Canal is now used principally for pleasure craft, including privately-owned boats, trip boats and even a 'Waterbus'. The only working boats are those used by BW for maintenance. The canal is, however, widely recognized as a significant local amenity and since the 1960s it has undergone some marked renovation. The piles of assorted junk that once predominated have been removed and the towpath is now a popular spot for those attempting to escape temporarily from the noise and bustle of city life.

The Walk

Start:	Camden Town tube station (OS ref: TO 289840)
Finish:	Paddington BR station (OS ref: TO 265815)
Distance:	3 miles/4½ km
Map:	OS Landranger 176 (West London)
Return:	For Camden Town take the Metropolitan or Circle line from Paddington to King's Cross and change to the Northern Line going north
Car park:	There is no specific car park. Public transport is both frequent and convenient and may be preferred
Public transport:	Tube from Camden Town connects to King's Cross, Euston, Charing Cross, Waterloo and Mornington Crescent

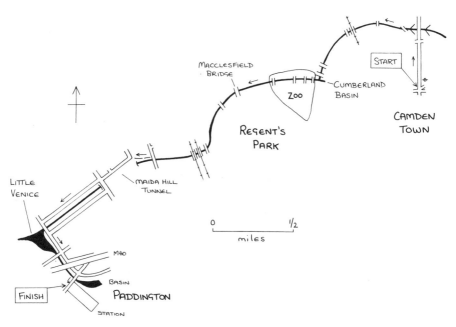

The Regent's Canal

Walkers on the Regent's should be aware that the towpath is open in winter between 10 am and 4 pm only.

Camden Town underground station has two exits. Take the right-hand one as you come up out of the darkness and turn right to walk up Camden High Street for about 1/4 mile. At the canal bridge, cross the road and go through the gate on the left-hand side of the bridge.

From a busy shopping street, the scene immediately changes. Within earshot of the traffic in Camden High Street are the vestiges of an altogether different age. The first thing in view is Hampstead Road Top Lock. This is the highest of twelve that run east towards the Thames at Limehouse, some 86 ft below this point. Until 1973 all these locks were paired to speed traffic and save water. Today, only this lock is paired. In the others one side was converted into a weir to help avoid flooding. The small, castellated lock cottage on the left was built in 1815. At one time it was a BW information centre and may be again one day. At the far end of the lock the canal is spanned by a cast-iron footbridge. On the near side a restored winch challenges the mind as to what it must have been for until I reveal that it was moved here from the entrance to the Lee Navigation at Limehouse, where it stood between 1866 and 1968. It was originally used to open and close one of the lock gates there and was put here by the Greater London Industrial Archaeology Society.

Hampstead Road Top Lock

Cross the footbridge to take the northern, right-hand, bank. On the far side of the bridge it's worth noticing the deep grooves in the stone and iron-work caused by the constant abrasion of barge towropes. The cobblestones on the incline, known as scorchers, helped give the barge horses purchase on a potentially slippery surface. Just after the bridge a doorway leads off to the much-renovated Camden Lock Centre. Opened in 1973 on the site of an old timber wharf, the buildings were once stables and hay lofts. The trade in timber continued here well into the 1960s, with the last lighter unloading cargo about 1969. Today the buildings house a variety of shops and cafés, and on a weekend an open market.

The towpath continues over the canalside entrance to the large railway interchange warehouse on the right. This entrance was known as the Dead Dog Tunnel for reasons perhaps not worth dwelling on. Here goods were transferred from the railway to the canal and there was a huge area of underground storage used for wines and spirits, popularly known as the Camden Catacombs. After going under Southampton Bridge, a watersports youth club known as the Pirate Club occupies the southern bank. Just beyond is a horse ramp, built so that beasts which had fallen into the canal could make a ready exit. The canal company claimed that the railways were a particular cause of horses bolting, although why this should be a problem peculiar to the Regent's is a mystery. Meanwhile, the canal moves quietly through the busy backstreets of Camden Town and under two railway bridges that carry Robert Stephenson's London & Birmingham Railway to the nearby Euston station. Stephenson had problems with these bridges, as both had to be built without interrupting the canal traffic. There was also a relatively steep incline up to the canal in order to provide sufficient head-room. As early locomotives were incapable of tackling the gradient, the trains originally had to be hauled into Euston by a stationary engine that was connected to the carriages by cable.

After the Gloucester Avenue Road Bridge, the scene changes again and the canal enters a stretch where the gardens of some stately Victorian houses proffer their greenery to passing towpathers. Ahead are two more bridges (Grafton Bridge and Water Meeting Bridge) before the canal reaches the outskirts of Regent's Park. These 410 acres were originally part of Marylebone Park, one of Henry VIII's royal hunting grounds. It was John Nash who, between 1812 and 1827, restructured them into the park you see today. It was opened in 1838 and named after the Prince Regent (later King George IV). At first it was planned that the canal would pass through the centre of the park on its way to Paddington. John Nash certainly thought well of the idea originally but local objections and the realization that the canal would be populated by uncouth bargemen forced Nash to re-route the line along the park's northern perimeter. This decision explains the sudden right turn which exists here at the north-eastern corner. As the canal bends right, the Cumberland Basin is on the left. What is today a mooring area, including the rather fancy floating Feng Shang chinese restaurant, was once a $^1/_2$ mile long arm that led off round the park to Cumberland Hay Market (although it also sold meat and vegetables) on the New Road near Euston station. The branch was filled in with rubble in 1948 and part of it sits under the zoo car park.

The canal now takes on the ambience of a royal park, with some fine trees and a pair of elegant cast-iron bridges. The first was made by Henry Grissell of London in 1864 and the second by R. Masefield & Co. of Manor

Ironworks, Chelsea. Between the two is another horse ramp. Beyond the bridges is the zoo landing stage of the canal Waterbus. The canal runs through the middle of London Zoo and, although there is no access, tow-pathers get a good view of some deer as well as Lord Snowdon's massive aviary. The 36 acre Zoological Gardens was designed by Decimus Burton and first opened to the public in 1828. Incidentally, the two upright stones by the side of the towpath mark the old parish boundaries of St Marylebone and St Pancras.

The canal continues around the park and under a footbridge to reach a fine-looking bridge with cast Doric columns. This is Macclesfield Bridge, so named after the first chairman of the Regent's Canal Company. It is also known as Blow-Up Bridge following an infamous accident in the early hours of Friday 2 October 1874. A steam tug, the *Ready*, was towing five barges from the City Road towards Paddington on its way to Nottingham. One of the barges, the *Tilbury*, was loaded with a range of goods, including several barrels of petroleum and 5 tons of gunpowder from the Royal Arsenal at Woolwich. Just before 5 a.m., a spark from the chimney of the *Ready* landed

The aftermath of the Regent's Park explosion, 1874. The remains of the columns, which were re-used when Macclesfield Bridge was rebuilt, can be seen in the bottom right-hand corner

Marylebone Public Library

on the deck of the *Tilbury*, igniting firstly the petroleum vapour and then the gunpowder. The explosion killed three crewmen, reduced the bridge to a pile of rubble and damaged houses in the vicinity. The bang was heard 12 miles away. The bridge's Doric columns were salvaged from the wreckage and were re-used in the new bridge. If you look carefully, you should see that the towrope marks appear, improbably, on both sides of the columns, showing that when re-erected they were turned round. The Grand Junction's carrying company eventually paid over £80,000 in compensation to more than 800 claimants, a considerable sum in those days.

The walk continues on under what appears to be a sturdy footbridge but is in fact an aqueduct for the River Tyburn, one of London's many underground rivers (it's even buried within the aqueduct). It was used by Nash as a feeder for his Regent's Park lake. Continue round the north-western fringes of the park, with many fine Regency houses adding an air of elegance to the route. A large house on the right is Grove House, also designed by Decimus Burton. As Park Road Bridge crosses the canal, the minaret of the Central Islamic Mosque can be seen over to the left. This is the border of the park and you should pass under two railway bridges, one part of the underground line to Watford and Amersham, and the other the BR line to Marylebone station. The Lisson Grove housing estate now dominates the left-hand bank as the canal bends gently right past a mooring site to St John's Wood Road. In normal circumstances it should be possible to continue through the short tunnel ahead. However, when I was here some repair work was being undertaken on the towpath. If this is still closed on your visit, take the pathway up right to the road. Cross and take the passageway to the right that passes alongside an iron-railing fence.

Whether on the towpath or on the footpath above it, the Maida Hill Tunnel is now directly ahead. Just before it is the site of the former wharf for the Marylebone (St John's Wood) power station. At one time this was a very busy spot as narrow boats were used to bring in the coal as well as to take away the ashes. The tunnel itself is 272 yd long and it is reputed that the spoil from its excavation was used as topsoil on the field of the nearby Lord's cricket ground. This was done because the canal passed straight through Thomas Lord's original site for the ground. The canal company also paid him £4,000 in compensation. There is no towpath through the tunnel so horses were uncoupled and brought up to road level to walk over to the other side. The men on the boat, meanwhile, would have laid on their backs on the deck and pushed against the sides of the tunnel with their feet to take the vessel through. An alternative method was a kind of inverted punting using a pole to push against the roof of the tunnel. Your route is somewhat easier. If on the towpath, go up the steps by the tunnel entrance to Aberdeen Place, which is where those who couldn't gain access have been for some time. Continue on along the course of the canal to Edgware Road

Junction House (the former tollhouse) at the western end of the Regent's Canal

where there are a small number of shops. Cross the road and bear right past a café into Blomfield Road where the canal re-emerges on your left.

A gate promises access to the towpath but doesn't deliver so continue along the pavement. The canal follows a straight course in-between two tree-lined avenues, each with some fine Regency houses. The line here is a popular mooring place and the gaily painted or plant-bedecked boats must make this one of the most attractive parts of town. The road culminates in a canalside cottage known as 'Junction House', formerly the Regent's Canal tollhouse, and the end of the Regent's Canal at the Warwick Avenue Bridge. The stop gates, once used to prevent water flow from the GJC to the Regent's, still sit in position under the bridge, although these days they are rarely closed unless for maintenance.

Cross the road to reach the Paddington Canal and Little Venice. This small lagoon is also known as Browning's Pool after the poet Robert Browning who lived in nearby Warwick Crescent. A good view of the pool and its island can be had either from the bridge or, if you cross the bridge, from Rembrandt Gardens. To reach Paddington station walk past the gardens and, following the signs, cross the road. The path passes under the massive complex of roadways and out to a small green where, by briefly turning right, there is a glimpse of the Paddington Canal as it sits underneath the

A40(M) overpass. To the right the line goes down to Little Venice, to the left on to the Paddington Basin. The basin was, of course, here some time before the trains and thus Paddington was an important inland port prior to the arrival of Isambard Kingdom Brunel. Many roads hereabouts still bear names like North Wharf Road and South Wharf Road in homage to a much more watery past. The basin is now fully enclosed and inaccessible to walkers, although there has been talk of redeveloping the area.

Continue on your original line to a huge roundabout on Harrow Road. Turn right into Bishops Bridge Road, cross this road and then turn left (again following the signs) into the rear of Paddington station. This is normally the taxi entrance but it affords a brief view left of the line of the Paddington Canal Basin. By following the path round, you will shortly arrive at the main line and tube stations to complete the walk.

Further Explorations

Virtually the whole of the Regent's Canal is open and towpathers can complete the entire line by walking from the Limehouse Basin to Paddington, a distance of about 9 miles. The towpath was much improved in the early 1980s under the aegis of the Canal Way Project and numerous information notices and plaques can be seen all along the canal.

Some of the most interesting features of the eastern end can be seen, however, in a shorter of walk of nearly 3 miles from the Angel tube station (Northern Line) to Camden Town. From the station, turn left along the City Road for about 1/3 mile to the offices of London Electricity, where you cross the base of the City Road (or Grand) Basin. This can be seen over to the left of an apparently pointless road bridge. The basin was opened in 1820 and was the most important of the canal's wharves, covering some 4 acres. At its peak the basin went beyond City Road but sections have been gradually filled in and the southern end is now occupied by office buildings. The basin was surrounded by factories and there were flour, timber and general trading wharves. By the turn of the twentieth century British Drug Houses (BDH) occupied most of the site. In recent years the old wharf buildings have been pulled down and new canalside houses built.

Continue along the City Road for a short distance and turn left along Wharf Road. After passing the rebuilt Pickfords Wharf, cross the canal itself and then turn left, just after an information notice, to reach the canal. Walk along to City Road Lock. From here walk on to the next road bridge, where you should cross to the left-hand towpath. There is now a good view of the 960 yd long Islington Tunnel. The tunnel was opened in 1818 and was originally a 'legging' tunnel. However, from 1826 the company provided a steam-powered tug which pulled boats through by working its way along a chain on the canal bed. This service survived well into the 1930s.

To reach the next stretch of the canal, you have to divert off the towpath and through the residential undergrowth. At the tunnel entrance walk up some steps to Colebrooke Row. Turn right and walk on to turn left along Charlton Place. Cross Camden Passage and then Upper Street. Go up Berners Road (with the Business Design Centre to the right), turning left and right into Bromfield Street to reach Liverpool Road. Cross to Ritchie Street and on, through a park, to Dewey Road. Continue over Barnsbury Road into Maygood Street. Walk on along an alleyway between houses to Muriel Street where the canal can be seen and a gap in the wall takes you back to the towpath.

Immediately left is the western entrance to Islington Tunnel. Further along, after some converted warehouses, is the 1½ acre Battlebridge (or Horsfall) Basin which abuts King's Cross station. St Pancras and King's Cross can be seen over to the left. You should now continue under three bridges and turn sharp right to reach St Pancras Lock, followed by St Pancras Basin, a coal wharf opened in 1870 by the Midland Railway. From there there is now just a short stroll on to two locks in close proximity, Kentish Town Lock and Hawley Lock. To reach Camden Town tube station (Northern Line), turn left at the next (iron-girder) bridge into Camden High Street.

Further Information

There is no Regent's Canal society as such but the Inland Waterways Association holds regular guided walks from Camden Town tube station. To find out the date of the next walk, contact the IWA head office (telephone number and address in Appendix B).

The most complete published description of the Regent's Canal is in:
Essex-Lopresti, M., *Exploring the Regent's Canal*, 3rd edition. K.A.F. Brewin Books, 1990.
However, there are sections on the canal in:
Hadfield, C., *Canals of the East Midlands*. David & Charles, 1981.

10
THE ROYAL MILITARY CANAL
Rye to Hamstreet

Introduction

The Royal Military Canal is a true oddity. Built at government expense in an impressively fast time, the canal, with its associated road and parapet, was designed as a military fortification against the rampaging French. Only after Bonaparte had decided to turn on Austria instead was the potential for commercial carrying considered. As such it never even looked like succeeding. It was, virtually from the day it was opened, a wonderful and notorious government folly.

The Royal Military Canal stretches like a necktie around the throat of Romney Marsh, separating that flat expanse of reclaimed land from the rest of Kent and Sussex. At its western end the canal reaches the sea at Cliff End, just 3–4 miles east of Hastings. From there it crosses the Pett Level to reach the orderly town of Winchelsea where, having joined the River Brede, the line continues to the Cinque Port of Rye. After winding around the base of the rock on which Rye sits, the line of the Royal Military then takes that of the River Rother to head north-east via Scots Float to Iden Lock. From here on the canal follows a new cut through Appledore and then goes more determinedly east past Hamstreet and Bilsington and on to the outskirts of Hythe. The final stretch of the canal is wedged between the town and the sea. It ends, in a rather inglorious way, on the sea front at Shorncliffe, just a few miles west of the centre of Folkestone.

This part of coastal Kent and Sussex has a peculiarly airy and remote feel, and in summer there's more sunshine than can be imagined. With a good pair of binoculars, a fine packed lunch and this book, you can easily lose yourself here (metaphorically speaking of course!).

History

In 1803 the brief truce between France and Britain (the Peace of Amiens) came to an end and the Napoleonic War resumed. With renewed hostilities came the fresh threat of invasion. British military experts saw the promontory at Romney Marsh as the most likely area for an assault, a figurative chin on the coast of Kent just waiting to be hit. The French punch was to come from Boulogne and was to be directed at Dungeness. The coastline around the town was almost ideal for beach landings and, despite the enthusiasm of the local people for fighting the French, it was a difficult area to defend. Between 120,000 and 180,000 French troops were reported to be awaiting the assault, supported by floating gunboats and other vessels that were to carry artillery, support supplies and some 6,000 horses.

By August 1804, the threat of invasion was at its height, and the new Prime Minister, William Pitt, was determined to improve the coastal defences. Although their efficacy was much contested, the first decision was to build eighty-six Martello towers as defensive forts along the south coast. A second, much vaunted, scheme was one in which the whole area of Romney Marsh would be flooded by the simple expedient of opening a

The line of the military canal around Rye follows the course of the River Brede to meet the River Tillingham on the southern side of the town, where this picture was taken probably about 1910

Hastings Museum

series of sluices. The suggestion for a canal as a military barrier against the potential invaders was made by Lt-Col John Brown, Assistant Quartermaster-General and Commandant of the Royal Staff Corps (a predecessor of the Royal Engineers). He had reviewed the flooding scheme and rejected it as impossible to implement. One report, for example, suggested that ten days warning would be needed, another that with a neap tide little if any of the land would be inundated. There was also the immense damage that would be done to the land; largely irrelevant if an attack actually occurred but severely embarrassing and expensive if the area was flooded as the result of a false alarm.

In a plan submitted to his chief, General Sir David Dundas, Commander of the Southern District, on 18 September 1804, Brown suggested that a vast ditch be built from Shorncliffe, a little under 3 miles west of Folkestone, to the River Rother north of Rye. The canal would not only be a line of defence but would provide the means of bringing up reinforcements to the threatened points, moving the troops either by barge or by the road which was to be made on the inland side of the canal. The road itself was to be screened from enemy fire by a parapet built of the soil dug from the canal works. The Commander-in-Chief, the Duke of York, approved of the scheme and agreed with Dundas that the line would not be without its commercial potential. The cost of construction was estimated at £80,000.

The speed of decision making was impressive. The scheme was forwarded to the Minister of War, Lord Camden, on 27 September. On the day before, however, the Duke of York had met with the Prime Minister to discuss the canal. Pitt was impressed by the scheme and ordered that the construction work should start immediately. The well-known canal builder John Rennie was appointed as consultant engineer and Brown was appointed military director. The following week, Rennie reported on his survey to the officer responsible for the direction and management of the works, the Quartermaster-General, Major General Brownrigg. In his report he praised Brown's original plan and suggested a sluice at Shorncliffe, culverts to carry flood water under the canal, and a navigational lock at Rye. Much of Rennie's efforts were expended on finding ways to remove excess water in winter and spring, and finding additional supplies for the summer and autumn. This was done by installing drainage pipes at the ends of the canal and by diverting some small streams into the line. It was also at this time that plans were circulated to extend the canal from the Rother through Rye and Winchelsea to Cliff End, about 3 miles east of Hastings. The ditch itself was to be 44 ft wide at the bottom, 62 ft wide at the surface and 9 ft deep. The extension beyond Rye was both narrower and shallower. A military road, running parallel with the canal some 52 ft to the north, was to be 30 ft wide and raised 3 ft above the level of the marsh. Rennie estimated the cost at £200,000.

To the east of Rye, the River Rother was incorporated into the military defences. This view shows the Union Channel junction, with the Cinque Port of Rye in the distance

William Pitt became personally involved in much of the organization and certainly assisted in convincing the local landowners to cooperate. At a meeting at Dymchurch on 24 October, he told them how the new canal would not only defend their country but would also act as a major drainage ditch for the winter months and a linear reservoir for the summer. This personal intervention won their support and agreement. The necessary land was handed over without recourse to the normal practice of valuation, haggling and legal document. Pitt's involvement in the project was such that locals soon started to call the canal 'Pitt's Ditch'.

The construction work, on what was then being called the Romney Canal, began on 30 October, just over a month after the original go-ahead and in the absence of any parliamentary authority. It was estimated that the canal would be ready by 1 June 1805 but virtually from the start it was clear that this was highly optimistic. Delays occurred which Rennie put squarely down to the incompetence of the contractors. However, difficult weather conditions and problems with flooding contributed to the delays. There were also misunderstandings as to who was actually responsible for what and as a consequence much of the work was inadequately supervised. By May 1805 the works were in severe disorder with just 6 miles completed, all activity stopped and the navvies dispersed. As a result, after a meeting between Pitt and the Duke of York on 6 June, the contractors were sacked and Rennie resigned. Lt-Col Brown was then given full control of operations. He took personal charge of the eastern end, with Lt-Col Nicolay in charge of the stretch from Winchelsea to Cliffe End. The project was henceforth treated as a field work under the Quartermaster-General's department. Work now proceeded much more smoothly, using military and civilian labour under the expertise of the Royal Staff Corps, who in 1805 were moved permanently to Hythe. The civilian labour on the project was paid 5s. 6d. a week and used mostly for excavation work. The soldiers built the ramparts and turfed the banks. For this they were paid just 10d. per day.

By 14 July 960 men were at work between Shorncliffe and Hurst: 700 cutting, 200 turfing the banks and sixty working hand pumps to keep the trench from flooding. By August this number had risen to 1,500. By the following August, 1806, the canal was open from Shorncliffe to the Rother. However, this stretch was partially rebuilt twice over the next couple of years. On 18 November 1808 a storm led to extensive flooding between West Hythe and Shorncliffe which washed away about 2 miles of the south bank of the canal. To prevent this recurring a strip of land between Twiss Bridge and Shorncliffe was purchased and the sea defences strengthened. On 9 January 1809 the regimental stores burnt down, considerably disrupting the work. The situation was made worse when, on 30 January, a storm coinciding with a spring tide, again saw a breach in the sea defences. This time the canal was filled with shingle and the Shorncliffe–Sandgate road was damaged. Despite these setbacks, the canal was virtually finished by spring 1809, although the defensive cannon, eighty Danish guns that had been captured at Copenhagen, weren't in position until July 1812.

The final cost of the Royal Military Canal was put at £234,310. This figure included £66,000 for land purchase and damages, which was still being sorted out in April 1807 when a meeting of landowners was held in Hythe. With accusations of profiteering being voiced, the government decided to put the whole matter on a more legal footing and passed an Act to establish the maintenance of the canal. The Royal Military Canal Act received the Royal Assent on 13 August 1807. The Act appointed commissioners to administer the canal. This illustrious group included: the Prime Minister, the Speaker of the House of Commons, the Chancellor of the Exchequer, the Principal Secretaries of State (including for War), the Commander-in-Chief of the Forces, the Master-General of the Ordnance and Quartermaster-General. One of the earliest actions (April 1809) of the commissioners was to reward John Brown with what must have been the princely sum of £3,000 in return for his good efforts. Brown was also made the director of the canal and provided with a house at Hythe.

By the time the RMC was ready, the threat of invasion had gone.

This print of Hythe from the canal bridge was first published in 1829. Apart from the bridge itself, it shows one of the passenger boats that operated between Hythe and Appledore, Iden and Rye at that time

P.A.L. Vine

Napoleon's plans had suffered a severe reversal at Trafalgar in 1805 and he was no longer in a position to assault Kent's chin. With the decline of the threat came an increase in the number of sceptics and cynics. Suddenly it was agreed that there never was a serious threat of invasion and that even if there was, that Napoleon's army would not have found the canal much of an obstacle. In 1807, almost in desperation at what was rapidly being seen as an appalling waste of public money, the government opened the canal to navigation in the hope of recouping some cash. The Royal Military Canal Act of 1807 enabled the commissioners to collect tolls. Only manure and produce of the owners or occupiers of the lands adjoining the canal was to be excused payment. The commissioners even owned a few barges of their own, sometimes towed by horses of the Royal Waggon Train (the predecessor of the Royal Army Service Corps). Over £84,000 was spent by the government between 1808 and 1809 finishing off the waterway, including covering the road and towpath with shingle, replacing twenty temporary wooden bridges and building a new bridge over the River Rother at Iden.

The canal was opened to the public on 18 April 1810. However, by then the line was already being used for a small amount of traffic. The wharf at Shorncliffe, for example, was busy as a landing place for timber and coal. The working canal was used primarily to carry shingle, sand, bricks, stone, timber and, perhaps almost uniquely for a British canal, a steady trade in hop poles. A convoy of army barges once did the trip from the Rother to

Hythe in 4 hours and at one time there was a regular barge service between Hythe and Rye run by a Mr Pilcher. The single fare in July 1818 was 7s. 6d. Obviously there couldn't have been much custom, for by 1819 it only went from Hythe as far as Iden and from 1822 only as far as Appledore. Even this truncated trip didn't last; it stopped altogether in 1833, seemingly because the RMC felt that too much damage was being done to the canal banks. However, a new boat may have continued operations during the 1840s. Tolls for use of the military road between Rye and Iden started on 9 July 1810, and between Rye and Winchelsea on 22 August 1812. Traffic in the first year after the opening of the canal for public use reached 15,000 tons, with receipts of £542. By 1812 canal receipts reached £576, and with road tolls and other income, primarily rents of canal land for sheep grazing, the total receipts were in excess of £1,000. Although the RMC's income reached a peak of £1,530 in 1836, traffic levels were never high and the government was never able to recoup its expenditure on the building and maintenance of the line.

The canal was thus never tested as a defensive structure. Certainly William Cobbett in *Rural Rides* thought that as Napoleon had succeeded in ransacking most of Europe he wouldn't have found too many problems with a 30 ft wide canal. Cobbett and others continued to grumble about the waste of money for many years and the canal soon became renowned as a kind of military folly. Its reputation wasn't wholly rescued until the late 1840s when both the Duke of Wellington and Lord Raglan commented on the strategic value of the waterway.

Although the planned military use of the canal was controversial, it had a major impact on the local villages. They now had a road as well as a water-way that allowed them to travel between Hythe and Rye, previously a tortu-ous trip at the best of times. The canal also provided drainage to the lands around Appledore, increasing the amount of rich arable land available and reducing the incidence of marsh fever.

In 1837 an Act transferred responsibility for the canal to the principal officers of the Ordnance (who controlled the Royal Artillery and the Royal Engineers). By this time the line was being looked after by an officer and sixty troops who were basically fulfilling roles more normally found on a conventional commercial waterway. There were twenty-one barges licensed to use the canal and able to carry between 21 and 38 tons. Annual income (£1,237) was sufficient to cover expenditure but a recent survey had shown that the canal needed extensive dredging if it was to remain navigable. The advantages of doing this can't have been very obvious to the officer in charge of the Ordnance, the Master General Sir Hussey Vivian. His view was that the canal was 'absurd as a means of defence . . . which ought never to have been dug'. This view clearly had an effect on the management of the RMC over the next few years, as a programme of what would now be called rationalization was implemented. The numbers of soldiers employed in maintenance work was drastically reduced and expenditure cut all round. Many functions, for example, were now filled by pensioners instead of sappers and at a much reduced cost. By May 1841 only seven Royal Sappers & Miners were engaged in work along the RMC and by October there were none.

The decline in traffic during the 1840s can be related to the opening of the South-Eastern Railway between Ashford and Rye, and, later, the Ashford to Hastings line. Coal traffic dropped sharply. From tonnage levels of 15,766 in 1847, cargo loads were down to 10,612 in 1849, with receipts halved. By now 60 per cent of the cargo was in shingle being taken inland to repair roads. The RMC increasingly relied on renting land to local farmers for sheep grazing. The average income from this source throughout the 1840s was £450–500 p.a. Two attempts were made to buy the RMC from the government during the course of the 1840s. The first, by the Hastings, Rye & Tenterden Railway Company, which wanted to convert it to a railway line, was defeated in Parliament. The second attempt was by the Lords of Romney Marsh and the commissioners of the adjacent levels. This proposal fell through when the Ordnance raised the issue of finance.

The outbreak of hostilities in the Crimea brought about another change of administration when the Secretary of State for War took direct responsibility for the RMC in May 1855. Among the first decisions to be made by the incumbent, Lord Panmore, was to reject another offer to buy the canal, this time from a Mr Smith. Although the present view of the War Department was that the line had little value as an effective defensive fortification, it would have at least the effect of being a modest hurdle for potential invaders. The key problem was that the government was now responsible for the drainage of the area and any relinquishment of ownership had to take that into consideration. In a survey in 1857, George Wrottesley proposed selling off the various assets, including, for example, the now fifty-year-old elm wood that grew along the banks of the RMC.

In the 1860s traffic along the canal continued at roughly 10,000 tons p.a. and income at about £1,200. This meant that there was a small but continuing loss on the venture of some £400 p.a. Thus, with no improvement in economics and a gradual disinclination to take the military purpose very seriously, the idea of divesting itself of the RMC grew more prominent in government circles. In August 1867 the Secretary of State was authorized to do so. There then followed a hectic series of exchanges. In February the *Kentish Gazette* announced that Seabrook Harbour & Dock Co. was about to buy the canal. In the end the War Department decided to give the canal away to anybody willing to take responsibility for the land drainage, and an Act to allow this was passed on 10 August 1872. The War Department was now able to agree to lease the stretch between Iden and Shorncliffe to the

Lords of the Level for a period of 999 years starting on 3 June 1873. The annual rent was to be a shilling. This was soon followed by Hythe Corporation obtaining an Act to purchase that stretch through the town for conversion into ornamental waters. In 1874 the War Department sold the canal west of Rye to four private owners. Meanwhile, the trade had all but gone. From 11,000 tons p.a. in 1867, traffic in 1887 was 158 tons. Despite a mini-revival in the closing years of the century, trade in 1903 had almost dried up completely. The last toll collected at Iden Lock was taken from the barge *Vulture* on 15 December 1909 for 27 tons of shingle.

The eastern canal is still owned by Hythe Council and used by local pleasure boats. The western end from Appledore to Iden Lock is owned by the National Rivers Authority. Interestingly, the parapet on the road side of the canal was not sold by the War Department until 1935 and even then was requisitioned during the Second World War, just in case the original purpose of the canal was to be tested after all. As part of the 1935 sale, the section between Appledore and Hamstreet was bought by Dorothy Johnston who then presented it to the National Trust. Today the canal is still in water and lengths are occasionally used by canoeists and other boats. The River Rother near Rye is used by water-skiers who tear around the tortuous curves near the sluices of the Union Channel. The rest is left to the birds and the towpathers.

The Walk

Start:	Rye (OS ref: TQ 919205)
Finish:	Hamstreet (OS ref: TR 001337)
Distance:	11 miles/18 km
Map:	OS Landranger 189 (Ashford & Romney Marsh Area)
Return:	Hourly trains between Hamstreet and Rye, including Sundays, on the Hastings to Ashford line (enquiries: 0732-770111)
Car park:	At Hamstreet station (free of charge at weekends)
Public transport:	The walk starts and finishes at BR stations

This walk can be shortened by using the BR station at Appledore for a walk from Rye of 8 miles. The drawback of this is that the last mile is along a relatively busy road with no pavement. Alternatively, park in the centre of Appledore and walk to Iden Lock or to Hamstreet, returning along the same route. The distances involved are then 7 miles and 9 miles respectively. Sadly there are no convenient pubs or shops at Iden Lock.

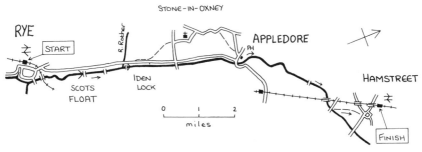

The Royal Military Canal

For the main walk the easiest approach from a traffic and car parking point of view is to leave your vehicle at Hamstreet and then take the train to Rye. Hamstreet station is on the A2070 Ashford Road just north of the intersection with the B2067. At Rye, leave the station to walk up a slight hill past some bus-stops to the post office on the right.

There are two minor diversions that you may consider worth taking before setting out. To see the River Tillingham and Rye Harbour, turn right past the post office. Walk down Wish Street, following signs for Tourist Information. Eventually this road leads to a bridge over the Tillingham. Here is the Tillingham sluice, a vertical gate that protects the land beyond from high tides. Just up from it is a smock windmill. A little further round on the road (with the harbour on your left) is a rather sorry-looking Martello tower. These towers were built at roughly the same time as the canal as part of the nation's defence against Napoleon. There were eighty-six of them altogether. This one was intended to guard the Tillingham and Brede sluices but is now dissolving into the surrounding scrap-yard. Turn left along the road opposite the tower and within 50 yd you will come to Brede sluice and lock, a large affair that protects the River Brede from the tides. The stretch which runs off right towards Winchelsea was, in 1809, the last part of the canal to be built. It was never used by commercial barges and, as it is much narrower than the rest of the canal, was thought by many to be not too serious as a defensive obstacle either. But of course by the time it was built the threat of invasion had subsided.

The second diversion is Rye itself. It's worth wandering through the unspoilt, if tourist-infested streets. There are a number of interesting places to visit and plenty of places to consume cups of tea. From the post office, go up Market Road to reach the town centre. Maps describing town walks are available in local shops or at the Tourist Information Office.

The walk proper starts at the post office. From the entrance, turn left to cross Station Road. Walk past a small Baptist church and the police station. Continue until you reach the massive town gate (Landgate). Turn right to go underneath and then bear left down a slope. Cross the road to pass to the right of the public conveniences and then bear left diagonally across the field to a road bridge across the River Rother. At the opposite end of the bridge, a sign for the Saxon Shore Way takes you left across the road and onto an embankment high above the river. The path continues to a railway bridge. This is the trickiest part of the walk as you have to go underneath it, a manoeuvre which could dampen the feet at high tide. Once on the other side, you realize that the walk has truly begun, with the Rother, acting as the Military Canal here, on the left and the vast, flat expanse of Romney Marsh to the right. The path now winds gently back and forth and passes over the sluices of the Union Channel, an important drainage ditch for the area of Walland Marsh to the east. After a further gentle bend, the massive Scots Float sluice and lock come into view. This is the tidal limit of the River Rother. The sluice that was here at the time of the building of the RMC was destroyed in a flood in 1812. Another was built here in 1831. The present structure dates from 1984. It's worth passing by the small brick hut to the bridge, where you can look at the sluice, formerly known as Star Lock, at close quarters. It consists of a pair of doors which open either way depending on the water levels. Boat owners wishing to pass through the gates have to give the sluice-keeper warning as there are occasions when there is simply insufficient water available to allow passage. This alone indicates that the key objective of the National Rivers Authority here is to prevent floods rather than permit navigation. In Edwardian times the sluice was the starting point for some early motor launch trips along the Rother to Bodiam Castle near Northiam.

To continue the walk, return to the right-hand bank, where a concrete road goes past the sluice-keeper's house and into a field. The Military Road, built at the same time as the canal to assist the rapid movement of men and artillery along the defence work, now runs parallel to the canal along the opposite bank. In just over 1/2 mile the path passes Boonshill Bridge to go over a stile and into a field. This then leads to the junction where the canal bears right while the River Rother bears left. The first bridge over the Rother here was completed in the spring of 1808. The present one dates from 1960. Iden Lock, to the right of the bridge at the start of the RMC proper, is the only lock on the cut section of the canal and was built entirely by the army, in fact the Royal Staff Corps under the command of one Captain Todd. It was 73 ft long and 16 ft wide with a pair of floodgates below the bottom gates to prevent excess water flowing back into the canal. Work on the lock itself wasn't begun until October 1807 and it was finished in September 1808 after severe problems with its foundations. Curiously, the quoin and coping stones were obtained from Dundee. The toll collector for the western end of the RMC was based here at Iden. Tolls were charged at 3d. per ton per mile for timber and 2d. per ton per mile for coal. Corn

Iden Lock at the start of the canal 'proper'

was charged at $2^1/_2$d. The lock itself was used regularly until 1902 and was last used on 15 December 1909. In the early 1960s it was converted into a drainage sluice by the Kent River Catchment Board (absorbed by the National Rivers Authority). Next to the lock, on the northern bank, is an original army-built stone lock cottage and, over the Military Road, are the former toll collector's house and military barracks, now a private house.

A well-trod towpath proceeds along the right-hand bank of the canal all the way into Appledore. However, as this is not a right of way, I am unable to recommend it. It is worth noting, however, that the National Rivers Authority is currently investigating its options and that Kent County Council has a long-term strategy to provide a linear route along the length of the canal. For the moment, walkers may consider crossing the bridge here at Iden Lock and then turning right to go along Military Road for the 3 miles into Appledore. After about $^1/_2$ mile, the canal shifts a canal width left from its rigidly straight line. A series of these zigzags can be seen along this stretch of the canal. The system, devised ironically by a French military engineer called Vauban, was designed to allow troops to fire laterally along the canal from gun emplacements situated at each double bend. One advantage of walking along the road here is that a better view can be had of the protective defence works that border the landward side of the canal. The embankments themselves were made from the soil dug from the canal.

For those walkers on the road who may wish to get off, there is a small bridge about a hundred yards or so after the first zigzag. This takes a path away from the road to Appledore via the Saxon Shore Way. The route is quite interesting but not always adequately waymarked. The first part may be particularly confusing. After passing over the bridge, turn right and walk alongside the roadside ditch until you pass the boundary stone which sits on the side of the Military Road (erected in 1806 to mark the boundary between Kent and Sussex). Here turn left and then right alongside another ditch. Eagle-eyed walkers, aided by a map, should be able to follow the waymarks up Stone Cliff then along the road to Stone-in-Oxney. Turn right at a T-junction and then, after passing a pub, turn right again into a field with a brook to the right. This eventually reaches a road near some oast houses. Turn right. The route arrives in Appledore opposite the church in The Street. Turn right to reach the canal. Walkers who walked along the road, or indeed those naughty people who stayed on the towpath, pass some further zigzags, Stone Bridge and a few more zigzags before entering Appledore.

Appledore is a most pleasant place, with pubs and a village bakery. Before the arrival of the canal, the village was surrounded by marshland and prone to outbreaks of marsh fever. The canal drained the surrounding fields, supplied the first road link with Rye and the west and thereby enabled the village to thrive. In the early days water from the marsh was lifted to the canal using windmills and, latterly, steam pumps. Nowadays electric pumps at Shirley Moor, Appledore, Warehorne, Ruckinge and Bilsington drain the marsh into the canal; others drain it into the Rother. In return, the canal acts as a kind of linear reservoir for the drier summer months. For many years there was a regular barge service along the canal between Hythe and Rye. The building by Appledore Bridge now used by Hayne's garage, was originally owned by the proprietor, Nathan Bates, who used it to house the barge horses.

Just across the bridge and through a gate is the National Trust section of the canal, with full rights of way along this left-hand bank. This 3 mile stretch between Appledore and Warehorne was bought in 1935 by an Appledore villager, Miss Dorothy Johnston, who presented it to the National Trust. The military road has been covered with grass and it is a popular spot for afternoon strolls. Here, next to the canal, are the remaining stumps of the Huntingdon Elms that were planted by the War Office with a view to producing wood for use in rifles. The National Trust has taken great pains to replace the lost elms (which suffered in the 1970s during the first wave of Dutch elm disease), this time with oak and ash. But at the time I visited here, it was the profusion of May blossom that astounded the eye.

The fact that the canal was still considered to be a viable defensive position in 1939 is witnessed both at Appledore Bridge and along the National Trust section of the canal. At various points Second World War pillboxes were built to guard selected points. One pillbox manfully guards the Appledore Bridge, and another attempts to protect both the railway and the road bridges at Warehorne. At the Warehorne Bridge, the first after the railway crosses the canal, turn left and then immediately right over a stile and into a field. Take a line which passes diagonally left across the field, just to the right of the nearest pylon. This path eventually leads to the centre of Hamstreet. Turn left over the crossroads to the railway station, which is about 200 yd along the Ashford Road on the right.

Further Explorations

Sadly, not all of the Royal Military Canal is open to walkers, a position which is both illogical and frustrating. However, there are at least two other short stretches which can make a pleasant stroll.

There is a good walk of approximately 4 miles return from the Hythe terminus of the narrow-gauge railway, the Romney, Hythe and Dymchurch (OS ref: TR 153347). There are signposted car parks near the station. The walk goes to the small village of West Hythe, with a return along the embankment on the northern bank (there are rights of way on both sides). Take the narrow path to the right of the RH&D station near a café. The early stages of the walk afford good views of the trains to the left and there is an opportunity to see some of Vauban's zigzags. On reaching a road bridge, simply cross to the opposite side of the canal and return along the raised parapet. There are fine views over the marsh and a number of picnic spots.

At the opposite end of the canal, it is possible to walk from Cliff End (Landranger Map 199, OS ref: TQ 886134) to Winchelsea. From Cliff End, a rough lane firstly takes the left bank to a gate. The path then follows the course of the canal north, passing to the right the Pett Levels, famous for their rich birdlife. Follow the canal until you reach a road and then turn left into Winchelsea. Afternoon tea will no doubt restore tired walkers to a condition suitable for the return journey.

Further Information

The canal has no society to guard its interests and so the best bet is to join the Inland Waterways Association. The local group (the South-East Region: Kent & East Sussex branch) will then send you details of its meetings. The address of the IWA can be found at the end of this book.

For those who wish to learn more about the history of the canal, the standard work is:

Vine, P.A.L., *The Royal Military Canal*. David & Charles, 1972.

For a less learned but highly enjoyable read look no further than:

Godwin, F. & Ingrams, R., *Romney Marsh and the Royal Military Canal*. Wildwood House, 1980.

11
THE THAMES & SEVERN CANAL
Stroud to Sapperton

Introduction

The Thames & Severn Canal must have seemed like a good idea at the time. The busy wool town of Stroud already had the Stroudwater Navigation which linked it with the River Severn, and London was clearly in need of a waterway link with the burgeoning industry of the midlands. A line between Stroud and the Thames was thus built with lots of good intention and hope of a brisk trade. Then came the setbacks. Firstly there were constant problems with the waterway itself, and on top of that some bright spark built a bypass in the shape of the Oxford Canal.

The Stroudwater Navigation runs from the Severn at Framilode, not far from Gloucester, to Wallbridge on the outskirts of Stroud. Here it joins the Thames & Severn Canal which travels up the Golden Valley via Brimscombe, Chalford and Daneway to the Sapperton Tunnel. After emerging at Coates the line continues east to Siddington, just south of Cirencester, to where there was once a branch canal. The main line now turns south-east past South Cerney to Latton, formerly the site of the junction with the North Wilts Canal, a link route to the Wilts & Berks Canal at Swindon. The T&S meanwhile passes to the north of Cricklade and, in its final stretch, runs almost parallel with the Thames to Inglesham, just a mile south-west of Lechlade. Here it joins the Thames for all points south-east to London.

On a literally freezing January day, the towpath between Stroud and Sapperton was surprisingly busy with families, couples, joggers and, of course, towpath guidebook writers. In other words, it's highly recommended.

History

With the coming of the 1780s, it must have been more than evident that the largest potential market in the country, London, was physically isolated from the ever-expanding industry and canal network contained within the midlands and the north. At that time the capital still received the bulk of its goods by sea, a route that was always susceptible to inclement weather or passing pirates. The advantages of forging a waterway link cross-country must therefore have been a great talking point among canal entrepreneurs around the land and it is no surprise to find that the people of Stroud saw some potential in the extension of their newly constructed Stroudwater Navigation.

The Stroudwater, which joined the mill town of Stroud with the River Severn, had been a messy affair in incubation. There had been various schemes since Elizabethan times and during the eighteenth century a number of promoters had started and then failed to complete the works. Eventually, in July 1779, the Stroudwater was open from the Severn at Framilode, 8 miles south-west of Gloucester, to Wallbridge on the outskirts of Stroud. The new waterway was about 8 miles long and had twelve broad locks. Although the line had obvious potential in local trade, the opportunity to make the route part of a through line from Staffordshire to London was, it was widely agreed, just there for the taking. The Stroudwater Navigation Company, at a shareholder's meeting on 12 April 1781, ordered a survey to be made for a new line between Dudbridge, just west of Stroud, to Cricklade, John Priddey reported back in the following August. He advised that the canal could be built but that a better route was from Wallbridge to Lechlade, a village further down the Thames, about 12 miles east of Cirencester. He also informed the company that a plentiful supply of water could be obtained at Cirencester.

By 17 September, when a meeting was held at the King's Head in Cirencester, the proposed new line had attracted interest from the midlands. Among the promoters of the new line were individuals involved in the Staffs & Worcs, the Dudley and Stourbridge, and the Birmingham Canals. These companies saw opportunities for carriage of Staffordshire coal and goods manufactured in Birmingham. In addition, the people of Bristol viewed the line as an important route for their own products and, of course, Stroud businessmen saw potential for significant local development. Robert Whitworth, a student of Brindley, undertook the final survey and reported back on 22 December 1782. His recommendation was for a canal of $28^1/_2$ miles, with a rise of 241 ft from Stroud to the summit level at Sapperton by twenty-eight locks and a fall from Siddington near Cirencester to the Thames at Inglesham near Lechlade of 128 ft by fifteen locks. The estimated cost, which included a

1¹/₂ mile long branch to Cirencester, was £127,916. In drawing up his plan, Whitworth made the canal broad enough to take 12 ft wide Thames barges. Severn trows, which were 15 ft wide, would be able to navigate as far as Brimscombe, a few miles east of Stroud, where transhipment onto the Thames vessels would take place. The reason for this rather cumbersome action was that the Severn trows would be unable to navigate through the Thames locks and would have to tranship somewhere anyway. It was thus cheaper, in terms of construction costs, to get that transhipment as close to Stroud as possible.

At another meeting of the promoters on 17 January 1783, enthusiasm was such that almost 80 per cent of the required finance was promised within just three weeks. With this the Act received Royal Assent on 17 April. It authorized capital of £130,000, with powers to raise a further £60,000 if necessary. Josiah Clowes was appointed resident engineer, with James Perry acting as manager on behalf of the committee. Interestingly, the funds were raised from London-based speculators and those associated with the Staffordshire & Worcestershire Canal. This fact further emphasizes the enormous interest in the use of the line as a through route between the industrial cities of the North-west and London.

Among the most daunting of the engineering works planned for the line was a 2 mile long tunnel at Sapperton. The only tunnel of any significant length that had been built at this time was the Harecastle Tunnel on the Trent & Mersey Canal near Stoke. However, Harecastle had been built to Brindley's 7 ft narrow boat 'gauge' whereas Sapperton was to be a full 15 ft wide. It's no wonder, therefore, that many experts, including those of the Thames Commissioners, questioned the wisdom of building such a structure and recommended the adoption of narrow boat width. However, the fledgling company remained undaunted and confirmed its decision to have a broad canal in September 1783.

The construction of the T&S was, mostly, trouble-free. The contract for Sapperton Tunnel had been awarded to Charles Jones, who, perhaps optimistically, said that he could finish the work by the beginning of 1788. By January 1785 the line was open from Stroud to Chalford, and by the summer of 1786 the canal up the Golden Valley to the summit was in use. A wharf and coal-yard were built at Daneway Bridge and were doing a brisk trade. At Sapperton, meanwhile, building work was temporarily halted when Charles Jones became insolvent with only about a third of the tunnel finished. Other contractors stepped in and on 20 April 1789 the first boat passed through this most impressive structure. Beyond Sapperton, building work began in June 1785. The area near Coates consists of rocky ground, identified by Whitworth as difficult to keep watertight. To counter this the clay puddling was put down in two layers, each 2 ft thick.

The summit level, including the Cirencester branch, was complete by the end of 1787 and was in use as soon as the tunnel opened. The entire canal

The northern portal of Sapperton Tunnel *c.* 1902, with the lengthsman's cottage intact
Gloucester Record Office, The Boat Museum Archive

from Stroud to Inglesham was opened on 19 November 1789 at a total cost of approximately £220,000. The moment was celebrated in the inns of Lechlade and with a huge bonfire party. Traffic was able to travel from Brimscombe to Lechlade in three days and was able to reach London from Stroud in under two weeks. The line was not, however, without its teething troubles. Among other things, there was an acute shortage of water and the unusual problem that the summit level hadn't been built level.

Although the canal was opened with celebrations, the proprietors would have viewed developments to the north with trepidation. In 1790 one of the canal's prime purposes, as a route for coal from Staffordshire to London, had been removed with the opening of the shorter route along the Oxford Canal. London to Birmingham along the T&S was 269½ miles. London to Birmingham along the Oxford was 227. With the opening of the Warwick Canals and the Grand Junction Canal in 1805, that distance was down to 137 miles. The T&S responded to this development by concentrating its efforts on making its line a major link between Bristol and the upper Thames. The company sponsored a survey for a line from Bristol through the south Gloucestershire coalfield to join the T&S near Cirencester. In another scheme, the company considered a new cut from Inglesham to join the proposed London & Western Canal (which would have run from London to Oxford). With the Bridgwater & Taunton and the Grand Western Canals, a line was planned which would have provided a navigable route all the way from London to Exeter. However, with the more obvious line promised by the Kennet & Avon, this plan foundered.

Another problem for the T&S was the quality of the river navigations at either end of the line. The Severn and the Thames were often impassable through flood or drought. The Severn situation was to be remedied by the construction of the Gloucester & Berkeley Canal, which would provide an artificial channel to Gloucester and to the Severn at Sharpness. The Thames, however, was much more of a problem. The Thames Commissioners did much to improve the river during the course of the 1790s but the T&S saw its prime hope in the construction of bypass canals. The most promising of these was the Wilts & Berks Canal. Although this had been proposed as early as 1793, it wasn't until 1819 that the North Wiltshire line was opened to give the T&S a bypass as far as Abingdon. The final link that would have given an all-canal route to London, the Western Junction from Abingdon to the Grand Junction Canal, was never built.

Arguably the most crippling difficulty for the T&S was the lack of water at the summit pound. Weighty fingers were pointed at Robert Whitworth's final survey when it was realized that the feeders to the canal, most notably the River Churn, the Boxwell springs, the Coln and a supply at Thames Head, were simply inadequate. Some serious miscalculations had occurred which nobody had spotted until June 1790. A Boulton & Watt steam engine was installed at Thames Head in September 1792 to draw water from newly-dug wells but problems with leakage led to the canal being closed over the winter of 1791–2 for repairs at the summit level. These problems, of course, would have paled if business had been brisk. But it wasn't. Trade along the line at the turn of the nineteenth century was, at best, moderate. The traffic was mostly in coal imported at Framilode and distributed to wharves along the Stroud Valley, to Cirencester and to villages along the upper Thames. Even with this, toll receipts were low. In 1793, with a mortgage and bond debt of £97,200 and share interest owing of £28,600, the company's finances were in a poor state. The interest on the debt was serviced by raising more debt and the situation reached a head in 1809 when arrears on interest stood at £193,892. An Act in that year allowed the company to issue preference shares alongside its ordinary shares and the company freed itself of debt for the first time. In 1809–10, a maiden dividend of $1^1/_2$ per cent was paid to owners of both types of share.

By 1810 both the Kennet & Avon and the Wilts & Berks canals were open, and competition developed for the Bristol to Thames traffic. It was inevitable that tolls would be reduced, as they were under various agreements in 1811 and 1815. In the first half of 1817 some 10,615 tons of goods were shipped eastwards along the line, of which 9,481 tons was coal, primarily from the Forest of Dean. The trade was peculiarly eastward-dominated: only 664 tons of goods, half of which came from London, were shipped westwards. Naturally, the logistics of this in terms of boats having to return empty or only partially laden, had a big effect on profitability. The new canals were, however, not all bad news. The opening of the W&B (connected to the T&S via the North Wilts Canal) meant that the troublesome portions of the upper Thames were avoided and, as a consequence, the traffic levels at the eastern end of the canal began to increase. There was even a scheduled fly-boat that operated between Gloucester and London. But increasing competition from road transport, as well as from the W&B itself, limited toll receipts. For the period 1814–20, average receipts were £4,477, while for the period 1831–7, average receipts were £6,375. This increase in trade was helped by extensive works on the upper Thames, including dredging and better worked flash locks.

In 1835 a proposed railway between Cheltenham and Swindon via Gloucester and Stroud forced the canal to take drastic measures. It sought, unsuccessfully, to sell itself to the Cheltenham & Great Western Union Railway (later bought out by the Great Western Railway). The new railway was fully opened, a matter which included the construction of a second Sapperton tunnel, in May 1845. By 1847 the number of boats entering and leaving the canal from the W&B was under half of that just ten years before. Railway competition was also being felt for other coal traffic and toll revenue dropped from £11,000 in 1841 to £2,874 in 1855.

In 1865 the T&S decided to turn itself into a railway between Stroud and Cirencester, quoting the Sapperton Tunnel as being a prime asset. However, a bill of July 1866 was defeated in the Commons and all thoughts of challenging the GWR in the Stroud Valley were lost. Edward Leader Williams surveyed the T&S on behalf of the Stroudwater Company in 1875 and reported that the canal was in a poor state of repair. Although the situation was denied by the canal company, a majority shareholder, Richard Potter, sought an Act in 1882 to close the canal and convert it into a railway. This action was fought by what became known as the Allied Navigations, a consortium of canal companies including the Stroudwater, the Sharpness, the Staffs & Worcs, the Wilts & Berks, the Birmingham Canal Navigations and the Severn Commission. On 27 February 1882 the alliance agreed to underwrite the operation of the T&S (cost at about £550 p.a.) and to manage it. With this intervention the bill to convert the line to a railway was lost. However, the valiant and unusually cooperative efforts of the canal companies came to nought when in 1883 Richard Potter secretly sold his shares to the GWR.

The GWR treated its new acquisition with scant respect, selling off property and allowing the canal to decline for want of maintenance. The situation reached a climax in December 1893 when the company gave two days notice for the closure of the line between Chalford and the Thames. This led to a hurried re-assembly of some of the Allied Navigations, together with other interested business folk. This new consortium successfully persuaded the GWR to give it the T&S free of charge in return for promising not to build a railway line on the canal bed. Under an Act of 1895, the county councils of Gloucestershire, Wiltshire and Berkshire and the urban district councils of Stroud and Cirencester formed a trust to operate the canal, with powers to raise £15,000 to render the line into a navigable state. The line was to be managed on a day-to-day basis by the Stroudwater. At the same time the Thames Conservancy spent some £20,000 on dredging its waters and rebuilding many of the locks and weirs.

Under new management, the T&S re-opened in March 1899, only to close again shortly thereafter through shortage of water. At this point Gloucestershire County Council took legal control of the line, still receiving subsidies from the members of the alliance and still managed by the Stroudwater. With great expenditure of local government funds (nearly £30,000 in all), the canal was re-opened, bit by bit, in January 1904. However, by now there was little interest in using the route and the phrase 'white elephant' was widely used. Eventually the reality of the situation dawned and the last commercial voyage on the T&S was undertaken in 1911. The line was kept in water until 1925 when the legal requirement for subsidy guarantees ran out. After some negotiation, it was agreed to abandon the canal from Chalford to the Thames in 1927. Although the Stroudwater company fought hard to maintain the rest of the T&S, this battle too was lost in 1933 and the canal has been closed to traffic ever since.

After abandonment, Gloucestershire County Council sold lengths to various local landowners. With this division of the spoils, the future of the canal looked bleak. However, in 1972 the Stroudwater Canal Society was formed (the Stroudwater had been abandoned in 1954) and this was expanded in 1975 to form the Stroudwater, Thames & Severn Canal Trust Limited. In 1990 this metamorphosed into the Cotswolds Canals Trust, with the objective of restoring both waterways for navigation. The trust has its work cut out as anyone who does the walk will discover. It will obviously have to surmount the original problems related to the leaky summit and an inadequate water supply, but it will also have to overcome the new problems of a derelict tunnel and large sections of over-built canal line. In 1976 the cost of rendering the canal navigable was put at eight million pounds. Today it will be even more than that and at the time of writing new engineering surveys are being undertaken. The clear objective, however, is inspiring the trust and it may someday once again be possible to navigate along this, the first inter-city route to London.

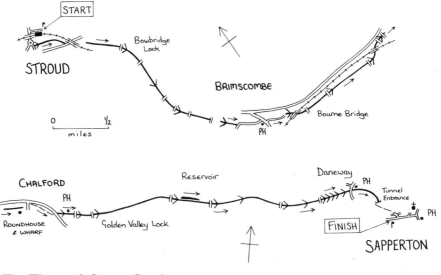

The Thames & Severn Canal

The Walk

Start:	Stroud (OS ref: SO 850051)
Finish:	Sapperton (OS ref: SO 947033)
Distance:	7¹/₂ miles/12 km
Maps:	OS Landranger 162 (Gloucester) and 163 (Cheltenham)
Return:	Stroud Valleys bus no. 64 from Sapperton to Stroud (enquiries: 0453-763421). No service on Sundays
Car park:	Stroud has well-signposted car parks and there is parking in Sapperton at the bus-stop near the school or near the church
Public transport:	Stroud has a main-line BR station

From Stroud railway station, take the road towards town and then turn left and left again to go under the railway. At the first small roundabout after the railway bridge, bear left to go past the Bell Hotel. Within a short distance a bridge goes over the canal. Sadly, the view to the right has been blocked by the new Bath Road. Formerly, apparently, it was possible to see the Stroudwater Navigation from here; the junction between the two waterways was just beyond a lock called Wallbridge Lower Lock. The navigation's basin and offices were to the left of the canal. Now all there is to see is a short, dismal length of canal, some scrubby concrete and the Bath Road.

Best therefore to get on with the walk by crossing to the left-hand side of the bridge and going down to the towpath which is to the right of the canal.

From the path the gates of Upper Lock can be seen. The decision as to which gauge should be used for the T&S was a tricky one. Severn trows were short and wide compared with the long and narrow Thames 'West Country' barges. Neither type would be able to travel the entire distance from Bristol to London without transhipment. The company could have decided on the use of a wholly new vessel able to undertake the entire trip but decided instead on building a special transhipment port at Brimscombe. Locks either side of Brimscombe are therefore of different sizes: all those to the west are built to take Severn trows, all those to the east built for barges. Upper Lock is thus a trow-sized lock 72 ft x 16 ft 6 in.

The area up from the lock is the site of Stroud Wharf, marked by the stone edging to the towpath and the old warehouse (built in 1828) on the opposite bank. From here the line winds around the outskirts of town. After going under the relatively recent Stroud bypass, the route seems to get lost as the canal disappears into a culvert. Follow the clear path that goes under the railway (the canal originally went beneath the steel span of the viaduct, though a restored line would go through one of the brick archways) and then go straight on with the road left and a wooden fence right. This leads back down to the left-hand bank of the canal, with the River Frome rushing headlong close to your left. Within a short distance, you reach the first of many mills to be seen between here and Sapperton: Arundel's Mill. This is marked by the presence of the sluice gates and an overgrown millpond. Like many of the other mills, when Arundel's was converted from water to steam power, it received its coal supplies directly from the T&S.

The path is now wedged between the canal and the River Frome. After going up and over a road bridge, you reach Bowbridge Lock. As at Wallbridge, the lock has been dammed to keep the length above it in water. To the left is a fine circular weir, and just beyond is the first of the many surviving T&S milestones which recorded the distance to both Wallbridge and Inglesham. The canal now bends round to reach Stanton's Bridge and Griffin's Lock. Above Griffin's Lock is Jubilee Bridge, an iron footbridge built in 1887 to celebrate Victoria's fifty years as queen. From here the canal heads towards Ham Mill Bridge and Lock which, like many along the way, are named after a local mill. This one is of note because here, in 1933, the last coal barge to be moved on the T&S was unloaded. A short distance further on is Bagpath Bridge. Just beyond the Hawker Siddeley works, you should peer into the distance to the left. The Phoenix Ironworks which once occupied this site produced machinery and lawn mowers but now the building produces books, as it is home to Alan Sutton Publishing.

From Bagpath, the canal curves gently south-east towards Hope Mill Lock. The lock has long since disappeared under concrete, and the road and buildings on top of it create just one of the major obstacles confronting the trust's restoration plans. The buildings to the right of the fenced footpath were formerly those of the Abdela & Mitchell boat building yard. A&M built a range of vessels varying from small sailing boats to large steam launches. The ex-mill buildings on the left were used as the offices and engine factory. A&M continued building here until the Second World War, even though the canal had closed in 1933. The part-built boats were sent out by road. Continue along the fenced path. The line of the canal shortly re-appears and 400 yd on is Gough's Orchard Lock, next to the once-extensive Brimscombe Mills. This extant portion of the line is short-lived and you soon arrive at a road. From here into Brimscombe the canal has been buried in concrete and brick. Walk along the road to a junction and turn right up Brimscombe Hill past The Ship (right) and alongside Port Mill (left). Turn left, following the advice given by the signpost, for Port Foundry. Here is a better view of the fine Port Mill buildings. The Bensons International car park to the left of the path was built on top of Brimscombe Port, once the headquarters of the T&S Company. It was here that cargo was transferred from trow to barge. Although yielding a healthy sum in port dues, this activity was a major obstacle to the smooth flow of traffic. The port consisted of a basin some 700 ft long and 250 ft wide which could hold a hundred boats. In the central area was an island on which goods liable to be pinched were safely stored. On the northern, left-hand, side was the principal wharf and the main T&S building, a huge three-storey house incorporating a store and office as well as homes for key staff. Also on that side was a transit shed, a forge and a boat-weighing machine. The building behind you (on the other side of the Frome) is one of two original structures that still remain. This was the salt warehouse. The stone building just inside the car park was another salt store. It is clearly impossible for the canal to be restored here and it is hoped that the River Frome can be used as a bypass.

To continue, follow the path which runs along the left-hand bank of the Frome. At Port Foundry the path leaves the river by bearing left to reach the canal at Bourne Lock. This was a hybrid lock, able to take both barges and trows. It allowed the trows access to the company's Bourne boat-yard which was just beyond. Above the lock, the railway swings back across the canal on an arched viaduct. The site of the boat-yard was across the canal to the left. The yard built barges and trows and maintained the company's working fleet of over fifty vessels. Boats were built in dry dock or on the bank and were launched sideways. The site has now disappeared under some post Second World War factories.

The canal now curves gently to Bourne Bridge where, on a site used by a body repair shop, Brimscombe Gasworks once received its coal supplies from the canal. After Beale's Lock and Bridge the towpath goes on to St Mary's Lock. In both cases the narrowness of the locks compared with those already past is noticeable. Just before St Mary's Lock is one of the few places where there is a connection between the canal and the Frome via a culvert under the towpath. Further on, just before the canal again passes under the railway, keep an eye open to the right of the towpath for a Great Western Railway boundary post. After the railway there is another, again on the edge of the towpath. The canal, meanwhile, goes on to Iles Mill Lock. Just after this the line is again filled in and four garages sit on top of what was once Ballinger's Lock. Within a short distance the canal reaches Chalford Wharf and roundhouse. These stone roundhouses are a unique feature of the T&S. There were five altogether: at Chalford, Coates, Cerney Wick, Marston Meysey and Inglesham. They were built as lengthsman's cottages in 1790–1. Each has three storeys: a ground floor stable, a first floor living room and an upstairs bedroom. The Chalford roundhouse, which was once a T&S museum, is now a private house. Why they were

The roundhouse at Chalford Wharf

built in this style isn't known, although there must be a good view up and down the line from the windows. Next to the roundhouse stands the former Company's Arms Inn, part of which dates back to the fifteenth century. Also on the wharf in front of the roundhouse is some old sluice gear from Sevill's Mill.

As Chapel Lock was infilled in 1964, the canal leaves Chalford via a culvert. The path leads out to cross a minor road. Go straight on behind a bus shelter and past Chalford trading estate. The canal now winds past the last group of mill buildings and under the A419. Here, bear left to cross the road (and the canal) to take a footpath that goes left opposite Springfield House Hotel. Now, with the canal to the right, walk on to pass Bell Lock and, later, Red Lion Lock, both of which were named after local pubs. The lock bridge for Red Lion Lock, about a hundred yards up from the pub, bears the inscription 'CLOWS ENGr 1785', commemorating the engineer Josiah Clowes and the date when the first commercial load left Wallbridge. Around the next bend is Golden Valley Lock. The Cotswold-stone house just beyond was formerly a millhouse, became the Clothiers Arms pub, then the Valley Inn and is now a private house. From here the canal leaves the village of Chalford to pass the large Victorian waterworks which received the coal

Bell Lock and the Bell and Red Lion inns, photographed in 1910 for a Frith & Co. postcard

Gloucester Record Office, The Boat Museum Archive

that powered its steam pumps by canal. The pound after Baker's Mill Lower Lock was one of those that leaked badly and which was lined with concrete in the 1890s. The current low water level reveals this rather nicely. Below Baker's Mill Upper Lock is Twissell's Mill, a cloth mill that later ground corn. The millpond and some of the surrounding land was bought by the T&S and converted into a reservoir. The new 'lake' is 900 ft long, 94 ft wide and contains three million gallons of water. It feeds the canal through a small culvert under the towpath just above Upper Lock.

After the reservoir there are two locks at Puck Mill. The pound between them was infamous for its leaks and water was said to flow out as quickly as it went in. Even in 1907, Gloucestershire County Council was spending vast amounts of cash relining this stretch. Temple Thurston comments on the lack of water during his visit in 1910: '. . . the draught of water is bad; in some places we just floated, and no more. . . . There were times when I thought the tow-line must give way, the strain upon it was so great.' At Puck Mill Upper Lock, the towpath changes sides. For a section above the mill site, the canal is constricted by the walls of Puck Mill Wharf. From 1927 to 1933 this was the eastern-most end of the canal. Everything from here up was officially abandoned in 1927 and the rest followed just six years later.

Whitehall Upper Lock, a surprisingly long distance from the Lower Lock, is the bottom of a flight of seven in just 1/2 mile up to the summit level at Daneway. In an attempt to limit the amount of water used to run these locks, major alterations were made in the 1820s and '30s. By then, 70 ft long narrowboats were replacing the 90 ft Thames barges. The T&S was therefore able to shorten the locks by 20 ft and reduce downstream water flow by about 20 per cent. At the same time, the top locks were all fitted with side-pounds, limiting water loss still further by retaining some of the water evacuated when the lock was emptied. The remains of some of the side-pounds can still be found amid the undergrowth.

The next lock is Bathurst Meadow Lock. The towpath changes sides and, within 300 yd, Sickeridge Wood Lower, Middle and Upper locks follow. At Daneway, the Basin Lock stands alongside the wharf and basin. Above the lock the canal opens into a winding hole with the wharf entrance to the right. The basin was used to unload coal, stone and timber, as well as being a place for boats to moor before venturing into Sapperton Tunnel. The concrete-lined basin also served as a reservoir for the locks down the valley. The small wharfinger's cottage has been modernized and is now a private house, while the wharf itself has been flattened. The canal reached Daneway in 1786, three years before the tunnel was finished. It thus became the terminus for the line and, with a wharf, warehouse and coal-yard, was relatively busy with goods being unloaded for Cirencester and beyond. Immediately after the bridge is Daneway Lock and the canal summit, a total rise of 241 ft through twenty-eight locks. Again the towpath changes sides and the lock itself has been infilled to form a car park for the Daneway Inn. The inn was built in 1784 as accommodation for the navvies working on the tunnel. It was sold in 1807 to become the Bricklayer's Arms and has been a pub ever since.

From the road, follow the footpath sign to Sapperton over a stile, into the field below the car park and back to the towpath. The line passes over the culverted River Frome, past a derelict watchman's cottage and into Sapperton Tunnel. The tunnel was by far the most important engineering project on the T&S. Started under contract to the incompetent and often drunk Charles Jones, the work had to be finished by others, most notably John Nock and Ralph Sheppard. In the late 1700s tunnelling on this scale was an unknown quantity. Even now there are only two longer canal tunnels in the country. At its deepest point the tunnel is 200 ft below the surface and, in all, it is 3,817 yd long. As was normal for tunnels built at this time, there is no towpath. Boats were 'legged' or pushed through by men who lay on the roof or prow of the vessel and who then walked against the tunnel walls. This process could take five hours eastbound, against the flow from the pumping station, and three hours westbound. As it wasn't possible for boats to pass each other in the tunnel, only three or four passages per day were allowed and then at specific times. While the legging was in progress, the horses or donkeys followed a path over the hill. The tunnel itself has been blocked since the First World War, the crumbling layers of fuller's earth and inferior oolite proving too unstable despite the brick and stone lining. Its restoration, still a key hope of the canal trust, will be technically possible but inordinately expensive. The portal here originally bore some fancy Gothic battlements and fine tall, pointed finials.

To return to Sapperton, go back to what remains of the lengthsman's cottage and go up the hill. This moderately clear path (aim slightly right of the church) leads over two stiles to the road and Sapperton school for either the car or the bus back to Stroud.

Further Explorations

Although the T&S has been closed since 1933, there is still quite a lot to be seen. Sadly, not all of it is open to the public, although some lengths of the towpath are rights of way. If you wish to see the entire line, arm yourself with an Ordnance Survey map and Handford and Viner's book and you should be able to make your way without trespass.

One easily accessible section is that leading to the eastern portal of Sapperton Tunnel. This walk of about 1¹/₂ miles starts in Coates, near the village hall. Coates can be found off the A419 to the south-east of

The Tunnel House at Coates near the eastern end of the Sapperton Tunnel

Sapperton at SO 978007 on OS Landranger 163. From the village hall walk back towards the road with the bus shelter and turn right. Go along this lane past another bus-stop. When the road bends sharply right, carry straight on along a fenced path signposted to the church. Go through the churchyard. At the lane turn left to go through a farmyard. Walk along the left edge of the field to another field. Here the clear path goes across the middle to a gap in the wall. Continue across the middle of the next field to a stile. Cross the railway to a stile and bear left along the lane towards the Tunnel House. To the left here is the eastern portal of Sapperton Tunnel and the T&S.

The Tunnel House, originally called the New Inn, was built by Lord Bathurst to house the men working on the tunnel excavation. The original building was burnt down in 1952 but has been successfully restored if on a slightly smaller scale. To reach the canal, cross over the top of the portal and turn left down the slope to the right-hand bank. The eastern portal is of a completely different design to the western. This side is much more classical in style, built of stone with columns and nooks for statuettes. Figures of Father Thames and Madam Sabrina were intended to stand on the portal but somehow never made it. Similarly, an inscription was never added to the space allowed for it; perhaps finding the right candidate for such an honour alluded them. What you presently see is in fact all thanks to some fine restoration work that was completed in 1977.

The waterway stretching out from the tunnel through the cutting was once known as 'King's Reach', following a visit to the eastern portal by George III on 19 July 1788. The king also had a quick look at the western portal and the canal at Wallbridge. Whether he walked along the towpath isn't recorded but that is your route back to Coates. The section of canal through the cutting was lined with concrete in the early years of this century in an attempt to stop the leaks. The path leads round to Tarlton Bridge and on to Coates roundhouse. This, like the one at Chalford, was built as a lengthsman's cottage in 1790. This particular roundhouse once had a concave, lead-lined roof that was purportedly used to catch water to top up the canal. This house also has a kitchen extension that was built at the behest of the incumbent's wife in the late nineteenth century. The ground floor, which was normally a stable, was converted into living quarters at the same time. Sadly, the Coates house is now pretty dilapidated.

The path continues under the railway line and along a progressively more overgrown waterway. Eventually the line dries up completely. At the next accommodation bridge, Trewsbury Bridge, go up the side and turn left. The track leads through a small farmyard and out along the right-hand edge of a field. As the wall bends left, go over a wall stile into a field. Continue now with a wall close left to another stile and a road. Turn left to return to the centre of Coates.

Further Information

The Cotswold Canal Trust aims to preserve what's left of the two Stroud waterways and to restore them for navigation if at all possible.

The Cotswold Canal Trust,
FREEPOST (GL 65),
PO Box 71,
Stroud,
Gloucestershire GL6 7BR.

Those wishing to know more about the T&S should read:

Household, H., *The Thames & Severn Canal*. Alan Sutton Publishing, 1983.

12
THE WEY & ARUN JUNCTION CANAL
Alfold and Loxwood

Introduction

Although the Wey & Arun Junction Canal is one of the country's lost waterways – in places it is no more than a dry ditch – it has as enthusiastic a group of supporters as any in the country. Many stretches have been cleared and dredged, new locks and bridges have been built and people talk about the canal as if all the hard work had an inevitable conclusion. And, to coin a phrase, why not? It is possible, just possible, that someday boats may once again navigate along an inland route from London to the south coast.

The River Wey rises near Selborne in Hampshire and passes via Guildford to the Thames at Weybridge. The River Arun rises some 30 miles to the east amid St Leonard's Forest. It flows to the channel at Littlehampton by Pulborough and Arundel. At their nearest points the two rivers are only 10 miles apart and have tributaries that are just 2 miles from each other. The Wey & Arun Junction Canal leaves the Wey Navigation at Stonebridge Wharf, Shalford and ascends via Bramley and Run Common by seven locks to a 5 mile summit level near Cranleigh. Here the canal crosses the Surrey/Sussex watershed 163 ft above sea level. The line begins its descent near Alfold where it winds through Sidney Wood to go over a tributary of the Arun by the Drungewick Aqueduct. From here the line runs south via Malham and Rowner to New Bridge near Pulborough where the canal joins the Arun Navigation.

This walk is more akin to a nature ramble than a canal walk but is none the poorer. Here can be seen the to-be-restored and the restored in close proximity and a fascinating view of the problems involved in resurrecting a waterway that has been derelict for a hundred years.

History

There were plans to make the River Wey navigable as long ago as 1621, and in 1651 Guildford Corporation obtained an Act which enabled it to upgrade the river from the Thames at Weybridge. The Wey Navigation, completed in 1653, was 15 miles long with twelve locks. It was one of the first rivers in England to be canalized and was used primarily to ship Surrey grain into London and to carry coal from the Thames wharves. Although fraught with financial shenanigans, the navigation was highly successful and made Guildford a major inland port. So much so that the line was extended by 4½ miles in 1760 via four locks to Godalming.

The River Arun has been navigable from Pulborough to the sea since the Norman Conquest. In 1544 Henry Fitzalan oversaw a series of improvements to the main channel to North Stoke (some 2½ miles north of Arundel), including the construction of twenty-nine gated weirs. By 1623 proposals were made to extend the navigable waters along the line of the river to New Bridge near Billingshurst. The line to the sea was improved in 1732 when a new channel and harbour were built at Littlehampton. In 1785 the Arun Navigation Company was established and it raised £10,000 to improve the navigation with two cuts, the Arun Canal between Coldwaltham

Even in the early 1900s the Wey & Arun Junction Canal was partly derelict. Here an early canal restoration enthusiast admires the southernmost lock on the line, Rowner Lock
The Boat Museum Archive

and Hardham, and a stretch between Pallingham and New Bridge. The improved line was opened in 1790, by which time the company was already issuing dividends.

A bill to link the rivers Wey and Arun was brought to the House of Lords in 1641. This was the first serious attempt in Britain to link one river with another by making an artificial cut. The bill proposed that the new waterway would take a line along both rivers with a 2 mile long junction canal from a tributary of the Wey at Cranleigh to a minor branch of the Arun at Dunsfold. The main purpose of the new line was to avoid the often impassable roads between the south coast and London. At a time when Parliament was busy with its own problems, the bill was lost. Much later, the success of the Arun Navigation prompted that company to consider extending its line north of the already canalized section at Orfold and New Bridge, and in 1791 a proposal was made for a line north-west via Wisborough Green and Kirdford to Northchapel. At an independent meeting chaired by the Duke of Norfolk in Horsham on 9 July 1792, it was decided to continue the waterway to Weald Cross, Slinfold and then to Farthing Bridge near the centre of Horsham. This scheme was surveyed by John Rennie who estimated the cost at £18,133. The plan came to nought when negotiations with the Arun fell through in 1794. Another scheme, proposed in 1798 by William Marshall, suggested an extension through Horsham to Betchworth and Dorking. This met a similar fate.

By the turn of the nineteenth century a waterway was open from the sea to Arundel for vessels up to 200 tons and for barges as far as New Bridge along the Arun, and to Midhurst along the Rother Navigation which joined the Arun near Stopham. The line did not have a towpath and barges were sailed or punted upriver. The journey from Littlehampton to New Bridge took 2 1/2 days and barges were constantly being held up by floods in winter and droughts in summer. The company itself was heavily burdened with debt and was unable to pay staff, even though dividends of 2–4 per cent were still being disbursed. The situation was resolved by Lord Egremont, who bought the company and became chairman in 1796. Egremont was keen to extend the line north, believing that there were advantages for the local population should a route to London be opened. Throughout these exchanges, the Wey Navigation was doing well. In 1801 the line carried 63,000 tons of cargo, an increase that was partly due to the opening of the Basingstoke.

In 1803 John Rennie surveyed and proposed a scheme for a canal to run from the Croydon Canal via Redhill, Crawley and Chichester to Portsmouth. The cost was estimated at £720,649 for a broad canal. Although the idea was presented to Parliament, heavy opposition and a lack of financial support led to the shelving of the idea. Rennie had a second attempt in 1810 with his Grand Southern Canal that ran from the Medway to Portsmouth via Tonbridge, Crawley and Pulborough. Although costing a similar amount, subscriptions were more forthcoming and the project only foundered because of a lack of confidence over traffic levels along such a circuitous route. Another plan, proposed in 1807, was the Portsmouth, Southampton & London Junction Canal, which would have run from the Basingstoke at Aldershot via Farnham and Winchester, then along the Itchen Navigation to Southampton. The cost was put at £200,000, which included a 2 mile tunnel between Alresford and Alton. Although subscriptions were raised easily, the scheme collapsed on adverse cost estimates, water supply problems and controversy over the business forecasts.

After all these comings and goings, it was left to Lord Egremont to further the Wey & Arun Junction Canal Bill. The scheme was made public at a meeting at the White Hart Inn in Guildford on 1 June 1811. The proposal was for a line of 17 miles to join the Wey and Arun Navigations from New Bridge, Wisborough Green to Stonebridge, Shalford. The new line would complete a 90 mile route from London to the English Channel at Littlehampton. Egremont had secured the support of most of the principal landowners involved, including the Duke of Norfolk, the Earl of Onslow, Lord Grantley and Lord King of Ockham. Subsequent meetings, both in Guildford and in Godalming, voiced support for the idea and a committee was set up to further the project with a petition to parliament. Josias Jessop was engaged to undertake the survey. In August 1811 the committee decided to go ahead with the project at an estimated cost of £71,217, rounded up in the name of prudence to £90,000. In proposing the canal, Lord Egremont suggested that some 1,200,000 tons of goods were shipped annually from London to Portsmouth and that it was reasonable to expect the canal to take just one-twelfth of this. The trade would primarily be in coal, Portland stone, groceries, chalk, lime, timber and manure.

By October 1811 some £51,000 had been raised, of which Egremont had promised £20,000. The issue was fully subscribed by 16 November 1811, with 132 shareholders. By May 1812 Jessop had undertaken a detailed survey that included some diversions at the behest of landowners. The survey included the diversion of the River Arun between Malham and Rowner where the canal would have otherwise crossed the river twice in half a mile, necessitating two aqueducts. The revised estimate was £86,132. Finally, after negotiations with landowners, the Act was passed on 1 April 1813. It enabled the company to raise £90,500, with an additional £9,500 if required. The Act authorized maximum tolls at 4d. per ton per mile for most cargoes, with 2d. per ton per mile for manure. Lord Egremont became the company's first chairman, Jessop was retained as engineer and May Upton was made resident engineer and clerk of works. The construction work was contracted out to a builder from Alfold, Zachariah Keppel. The canal was to be 30 ft wide and consist of twenty-three locks, each measuring

75 ft by 12 ft, able to accommodate barges carrying 50 tons. Part of the water supply to the line was to come from a new reservoir built in the grounds of Vachery House, Cranleigh.

Almost as soon as the work began, landowners held out for independent arbitration on the value of the lands being bought by the company and the estimates of any damages caused during the construction phase. As the commissioners were themselves mostly landowners, some element of bias might be supposed and the company found itself spending far more than planned for both land purchase and compensation. Overall, this took over a quarter of the final cost of the W&A.

The first sod was cut at Shalford in July 1813 and work started at the southern end in the following May. The undertaking seems to have gone well up to the point where Zachariah Keppel became bankrupt after suffering some kind of cash-flow crisis. The winter of 1814 was also a very wet one, virtually stopping the work that was now under the supervision of May Upton. A further problem occurred at the Alfold cutting, which was found to pass through beds of sand and thus needed additional lining. The first tolls were taken at Bramley on 18 December 1815 but by this time funds were running short. With extra funds from two 'final' calls on shares, the work was finished in August 1816. The completed line was $18^1/_2$ miles long and the company had spent £102,626. The official opening on 29 September was marked with celebration that began at the Compasses Inn at Alfold and continued with a procession of barges up the line to Guildford. The celebration must have continued in Guildford where the price of coal fell by 20 per cent.

From the outset traffic along the canal was desultory. The average receipts for the first seven years of trading were £1,275 p.a., with less than 10,000 tons of cargo: just one-twelfth of the one-twelfth that Lord Egremont had expected. This figure appears even smaller when it is seen that the W&A carried less than half of that carried on the Arun Navigation. The disadvantages in having to tranship goods at Littlehampton, only to suffer the problems of going along the often impassable stretches of the upper Arun, made the sea passage to London look very attractive. The inland route proved more expensive with similar journey times. With the end of the war with France, the safety of the coastal route had also much improved, thereby encouraging coasters to make the trip. The lack of canalside industry cannot have helped matters. Even the W&A's initial success in delivering coal to Guildford was lost when the Wey Navigation reduced its tolls to make supplies from the Thames cheaper. As a consequence the W&A was unable to pay dividends for any of its first five years of operation. Despite these drawbacks and the generally low level of business, the canal carried seaweed to local farms, grain to watermills, and coal, groceries and merchandise inland from the coast. The boats returned with farm produce, timber, bark, flour and various rural goods. Chalk, clay, sand and gravel were also moved along the line. With the prospect of the Portsmouth & Arundel Canal completing the route from London to Portsmouth (the Act was passed in 1817), a small dividend was paid in 1821, but as this extension of the Arun Navigation did not open until 1828 this act of generosity using borrowed funds was not repeated. Instead the company set about encouraging trade through toll reductions and by signing agreements with the Wey and Arun navigations and the P&A in order to reduce the cost of carrying cargo from the coast to the Thames. This action, however, failed to produce the hoped for increase in business and in 1823 more toll reductions had to be made. Part of the problem was in navigating the Arun in periods of flood or drought. Even in good conditions the shallowness of the river meant that barges could not exceed 30 tons. After some pressure, the Arun company made improvements to its waterway so that by 1825 barges carrying loads of 40 tons could pass from Littlehampton to Guildford.

The opening of the P&A provided some improvement in the toll revenue. Income increased by 60 per cent to £1,989 in 1824. By 1826 receipts were £2,355 and a dividend of 1 per cent was announced. However, with the failure of the P&A (see below), toll receipts promptly fell by 20 per cent. There was some recovery during the 1830s, which saw good levels of trade throughout the Thames to Portsmouth lines. The Wey, for example, carried 86,000 tons of cargo in 1838 and the Arun paid a 12 per cent dividend. The W&A could only pay 1 per cent but maintained tonnage at around 20,000 p.a. (receipts peaked at £2,525 in 1839–40). By this time a £100 share was selling for £25 but at least the drop in value had been halted. The canal was still paying off its debt throughout the 1830s and it wasn't until 1842 that it was freed from this burden. Among the business on the canal at this time was coal from South Wales, imported via Arundel and delivered to Cranleigh and Bramley. The return cargo was primarily timber and stone. There were also fly-boats from Portsmouth to London.

By the 1840s the improved condition of the highways in Surrey and Sussex meant that road transport was beginning to have an impact on toll receipts on the W&A. Trade was beginning to drop rapidly: down 38 per cent between 1839 and 1840 and 1842–3, and over 65 per cent by 1851–2. The first railway in the region was the London to Brighton line, opened in September 1841. A line to Guildford and Godalming (opened in 1844 and 1849 respectively) reduced the receipts on the Wey Navigation by over 50 per cent. On 8 June 1846 a railway line from Shoreham to Chichester was opened, leading almost immediately to the total demise of the eastern half of the P&A. In 1850 the main cargoes carried on the W&A were coal (50 per cent) and timber (25 per cent) but by this time the total traffic was down to 15,121 tons p.a., with toll receipts of £1,036.

With the advent of a direct railway from London to Portsmouth, it was widely rumoured that the W&A would sell out to a railway company. Although this proved to be groundless, by the time the through line was built in 1859, traffic along the W&A was only maintained by reducing toll rates. The building of the Mid-Sussex Railway (Horsham to Midhurst) helped keep the wolf from the door for a while as some of the required materials were shipped by both the W&A and the Arun Navigation. But with completion of the Horsham to Guildford Direct Railway (which became the London, Brighton & South Coast Railway) on 2 October 1865, the W&A was forever bypassed. Indeed, it is this line that runs parallel with the W&A from Shalford to Cranleigh. So it was that in 1865 the last dividend of the W&A was paid. By 1866–7 the amount of cargo carried had nearly halved (in just two years) to 8,750 tons p.a. Cargo that went virtually straight away to the railway included coal deliveries to Cranleigh and the shipment of charcoal from Run Common.

At the W&A Annual General Meeting in May 1866, it was resolved that the company had no option but to dispose of its property. It owned over 200 acres of land, some cottages and other buildings. The intention was to wind up the company. However, at a meeting in October 1866, the motion to do so was rejected, primarily because a number of bargeowners had been buying up shares and were thus able to rally support to keep the waterway open. In response, a scheme was launched in which the Arun Navigation agreed to subsidize the line at £120 p.a. and to take responsibility for day-to-day management. Even this failed. On 11 January 1867 a poorly attended meeting decided to reject the proposal and resolved to go into voluntary liquidation. The closure of the canal was enabled by Parliament on 31 July 1868. With various rescue schemes coming to nought, the chattels were auctioned on 30 August 1870, although there was no bid for the canal line itself. This last hope having passed, the canal was officially closed to traffic on 22 July 1871. In the subsequent years it was run by the liquidator, with small portions gradually being sold off to local landowners. By 1901 all but eight of the 200 acres of the line had been sold and the company was eventually dissolved in 1910.

Meanwhile, the Arun was undergoing similar traumas. In 1882 toll receipts dipped below £100. Despite voluntary contributions from the proprietors, on 1 January 1888 closure notices were posted. The line was finally wound up on 23 September 1896. The fortunes of the Wey also declined towards the end of the century but, during the 1920s the Wey was carrying 55,000 tons p.a. and remained busy until the Second World War. Even in 1956 traffic was still using the navigation, with 16,105 tons being carried. The continuing decline eventually prompted the owner, Harry Stevens, to donate the line to the National Trust in 1963. Commercial traffic on the Wey ceased in 1969.

Even though the canal restoration movement grew following the establishment of the Inland Waterways Association, attention has never been overly focused on the W&A. Widely regarded as too far gone, the more immediate projects of the Kennet & Avon and the Basingstoke canals have been far more attractive. Despite this, the W&A has always had a band of enthusiasts. This initially small group, started in 1970 with the formation of the W&A Canal Society with, appropriately, Lord Egremont as its president. The Canal Trust (as it became in 1973) has raised funds, rebuilt locks and discussed the possibility of re-opening the line with the forty-two landowners involved. The northern end near Bramley in particular is a problem. The area is now heavily built-up and a new line will have to be sought. The hope of restoration is getting brighter but it will make the resurrection of the Basingstoke seem simple.

The Walk

Start and finish:	Alfold (OS ref: TV 038340)
Distance:	8¹/₂ miles/13¹/₂ km
Maps:	OS Landranger 186 (Aldershot & Guildford) and 187 (Dorking, Reigate & Crawley)
Car park:	Near The Crown in the centre of Alfold
Public transport:	None convenient

This circular walk goes firstly along a stretch of the abandoned canal and then a section under restoration. The return route is away from the canal and through the leafy Sussex and Surrey countryside. Casual towpathers should note that sections along the abandoned canal can be very muddy.

Alfold is a village on the B2133 that runs south from the main A281 Horsham to Guildford road. There is a limited space for car parking around the village green next to The Crown pub and St Nicholas' church. From the green, walk away from the B2133 towards the church. Bear right along Rosemary Lane to pass the Old Rectory and Linden Farm. This pleasant country road passes through some arable and then some wooded areas to reach Velhurst. A little further on, the lane reaches a fine house with some stabling. Here is a notice announcing Sidney Wood Farm and a small bridge (although it is called High Bridge) that once passed over the Wey & Arun.

By looking first to the right, the course of the canal can be seen disappearing into the middle distance. This line can be followed north by turning right just before the house and going into the Sidney Wood. However, the walk turns left just after the bridge to follow a bridleway sign which points along the right hand bank of the completely overgrown canal bed. There were once a total of six locks between here and the Onslow Arms at Loxwood (the Sidney Wood section as a whole had ten in just over 2 miles

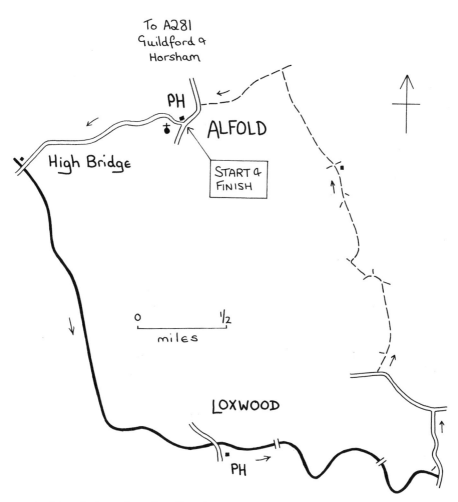

The Wey & Arun Junction Canal

for a descent of almost 90 ft). Sadly, most of these have now disappeared into the undergrowth. This, it seems, is partly a result of a certain degree of brick plundering just after the First World War and partly because what was left was blown up by the army for demolition practice during the Second World War. There was one lock, No. XII, not far in from High Bridge, although I wasn't able to find any trace of it. For avid lock-searchers, a sure sign of the positioning of any lock is a point where the canal channel becomes unusually deep and then the towpath passes down a moderately steep slope to meet it. But with the canal having closed in 1871 and the army having successfully completed their exercises, little or nothing remains

The Onslow Arms, a former favourite stopping place for passing boaters, at Loxwood

at some points and each individual lock needs some finding.

It's not all bad news though! The canal bed is now a fine area for wildlife. There are abundant rabbit holes and a wide variety of song birds. At one point, in early June, the sides of the canal bed were covered in early purple orchid. And if you loiter for a moment, the peace and quiet engulf you, a rare commodity indeed in southern England. In the days when the canal was operational, the loneliness of the wood wasn't missed by a number of locals who saw their opportunity. Passing barges were often subject to casual theft. One Alfold schoolmaster, for example, had a penchant for stealing duty-paid spirits as they made their way along the canal!

Using the criteria described earlier, Lock X is detectable as the towpath slopes down to a spot where there is a break in the canal wall to a dried-up lake bed. This lock, in the middle of Gennet's Wood, was severely damaged in 1841 by Charles Baverstock, who ran his barge into its gates. The resulting rebuilding and closure of the canal cost the company about £225. Baverstock was charged with negligence and fined £2 14s. After passing through a gate, a footbridge goes over the canal near Sydney Farm. Lock IX was, apparently, just before the bridge. Continue along to a signpost where another footpath crosses the canal. The footpath continues along the right bank, through a series of gates to a point where a dirt road crosses the canal to a house at Gennet's Bridge. Lock VIII was just before the bridge.

The act of passing down the Sidney Wood Locks was described in J.B. Dashwood's cruising guide of the 1850s as the 'great grind of the trip'. The book records that as each pound had to be left empty, downstream passage could be remarkably slow. The quickest method of passing through was to have two winches and to send a companion running on ahead to get the next lock ready for entry.

An old lock gate lies rotting in the mud at Brewhurst Lock near Loxwood

The metal quoins of the next lock (VII Southland) are still extant and thus give the first certain sighting of one of the Sidney Wood six. The lock gates worked against the quoins which were made of forged steel in 1814. The path now runs by an open field to the right, through which a footpath (from Ifold) comes to join the towpath. The canal bends left to reach a brick bridge, Devil's Hole Bridge. The stone walls of Devil's Hole Lock (VI) are, perhaps remarkably, in reasonable condition and can be seen from the bridge. The bridge itself was rebuilt recently by a combination of the West Sussex County Council and Loxwood Parish Council Youth Opportunities Project. Shortly after this, the path broadens to a dirt track which leads to a road, the B2133, and Loxwood. To the left is the site of the former Loxwood Wharf. Barges brought seaweed and lime, coal and gravel here and took away farm produce, timber and grain. To the right is the Onslow Arms. The pub was very popular with boatmen as it was the only stopping place between Bramley and Pulborough. The Earl of Onslow was one of the promoters of the original W&A bill. The pub that bears his name is recommended by CAMRA in the *Good Beer Guide*. The path continues on across the road and alongside a restored section of the canal bed. Within a short distance, this reaches Brewhurst Lock (V), derelict but definitely recognizable. The line of the canal from here on has received significant amounts of attention from the Wey & Arun Trust. Indeed, this section of the line has been leased by the trust for restoration purposes. It's worth noting as you pass Brewhurst Mill that in the original plans, the line of the canal would have turned north here via central Alfold to a point about a mile north of Alfold Crossways and would not have followed the route through Sidney Wood. The route was diverted to avoid Alfold village and various game reserves. It added 1½ miles to the length and £15,000 to the cost.

The activity of the canal trust is well demonstrated at the next lock, Baldwin's Knob Lock (IV), named after a local hillock. Here extensive renovations have been undertaken. The forged steel quoins are the originals but the masonry has been considerably reworked, as have the gates and culverts. Continue round the contours and along a wooded section that goes past a beautifully restored bridge and on into open country. The canal here was full and the whole scene idyllic. The sadness comes when one realizes how isolated it is from the rest of the waterway. The extant canal comes to a stop in the middle of a field. The original line went slightly right of centre and over the stream via the Drungewick Aqueduct. The aqueduct, which was demolished in 1957, was not one of the canal system's most ornate, being a rather heavy, even clumsy-looking, brick structure with three diminutive arches. Some canal trust volunteers at Baldwin's Knob Lock informed me that the aqueduct will be replaced by a steel channelled version faced with either stone or brick.

The towpath right of way comes to an end before the stream. To return to Alfold you should now take a route which leaves the canal. If you prefer, you can return to Loxwood and turn right to walk along the road. Alternatively, you could just walk back the way you came. The return route that I took keeps away from roads where possible but has no canal interest.

Bear left through a gate and turn left along a lane. At a T-junction, turn left. As the road bends left, there is a small side lane to the right. Go along this and turn right at the end along a bridleway. Continue past a sign for Pallinghurst Estate and along a path to the left of a gate. Go over a cross track and on through woods with fields to the left. At a T-junction, turn left to pass footpaths to right and left. The bridleway bends right and passes another footpath off to the left. Cross two dirt road junctions to reach a spot where there is a rash of footpath signs. Here go straight on through a gate to join the Sussex Border Path. This goes past a pond into an open area. Bear left through a gate and along a path with open fields to the left. After passing an attractive farmhouse, you will reach a wide dirt lane. Turn left. Follow the course of this track to reach a road and then turn left into Alfold.

Further Explorations

A walk from Guildford to Amberley along the Wey, the W&A and the Arun has been devised and is known as the Wey–South Path. As large sections of the waterway are not open to the public, the walk sometimes leaves the canal line but stays as close as possible throughout. The official route is 36 miles long. If you then follow the right of way along the River Arun to Littlehampton you will add an extra 13 miles. It could perhaps be managed over three full days. A description of the Wey–South Path can be found in Aeneas Mackintosh's booklet of the same name, available from the W&A Canal Trust (address below).

Not included in the Wey–South Path but well worth attention is the Chichester Canal. The Portsmouth & Arundel Canal Act, of which the Chichester was a constituent part, was passed in July 1817. The line was surveyed by Netlam and Francis Giles under the supervision of John Rennie. As with the W&A, the principal shareholder was Lord Egremont. The canal was in two sections: Chichester and Portsea. The Chichester line, a barge canal of 12 miles, ran from the River Arun at Ford through Yapton and Barnham to Hunston (where a branch of $1^1/4$ miles went into Chichester), then to Birdham and Chichester Harbour. Barges for Portsmouth were then taken 13 miles around Thorney and Hayling Island to the Portsea Canal which took boats $2^1/2$ miles into Portsmouth. An additional cut across the neck of Portsea Island to give access to Portsmouth Harbour (the Cosham cut) was added later. Following the passage of an amendment Act of 1819, the line from Birdham to Chichester was built as a ship canal, able to take vessels carrying up to 100 tons.

Despite initial enthusiasm for what was the final part of the London to Portsmouth canal route, investment was hard to find and only the combined action of Lord Egremont's wallet and Government Exchequer Bills enabled the project to go ahead. The Chichester Canal (Chichester to Birdham) officially opened on 9 April 1822, the Portsea on 19 September 1822. The whole line, including the Ford to Hunston section, was finally opened for traffic on 26 May 1823. It had cost £170,000. A barge could now make the trip between London and Portsmouth, a distance of 116 miles, in four days. The P&A was never a success. The most prosperous year was 1824, when 3,650 tons of cargo were carried against the predicted 55,000 tons. Expected government contracts for London to Portsmouth navy traffic didn't materialize. The reason was simple. Outside of wartime, the sea route was easier and quicker.

In 1825 trade halved and by 1826 it virtually disappeared with the collapse of the Portsmouth Barge Company. In the same year Lord Egremont severed his connection. An Act of 1828 enabled the raising of a further £50,000, which was used to complete the Cosham cut and to make good parts of the line that were already in disrepair. In addition, there were toll reductions, promotions of passenger traffic and a new carrying business. With this, traffic in 1833 rose to 2,500 tons, comprising mostly foodstuffs for the navy. Disappointingly, by 1838 the level was down to 750 tons. In September 1840 the last barge to sail from Chichester to London carried 6 tons of groceries. By the time the Shoreham to Chichester railway opened on 8 June 1846, the eastern end of the Chichester Canal from Hunston to Ford was already derelict and by 1853 it fell into disuse. By 1867 the line from Hunston to the Arun was reported as being 'quite dry' and various lengths sold. The P&A was eventually wound up on 3 November 1896. Various parts were then sold, although the line between Chichester and Birdham was presented to Chichester Corporation. With the turn of the twentieth century, traffic along the last remaining section dropped and was gone by 1906. In 1924 two bridges were culverted and on 6 June 1928 the corporation abandoned the line. A short section near the sea was re-opened in 1932 for yacht mooring but the rest was allowed to deteriorate. It was sold to West Sussex County Council in 1957, leased to anglers in 1972 and taken over by the Chichester Canal Society in 1984. With this, new hope has arisen, with plans to restore the canal to a navigable state.

Although the section from Hunston to Ford has long been closed, there is a good walk between Chichester and the yacht basin at Birdham. The walk starts at Chichester BR station. Go over the level-crossing along Stockbridge Road to the Richmond Arms. Here turn right along Canal Wharf to reach Southgate Basin, the terminus for the Chichester arm of the P&A. A public footpath sign points round the back of the pub and along the right-hand bank of the canal. The walk starts noisily as you go past Padwick Bridge and under the Chichester bypass. But gradually you enter the peaceful arable land to the south of the city. About a mile after the bypass, the canal reaches Hunston, where the towpath is forced left over a footbridge. Turn right at the end of the bridge to walk along the road for a short distance and then back onto the left-hand bank of the canal. This sudden 90 degree right turn appears peculiar but marks the spot where the Chichester arm joined the P&A proper. The line of the P&A ran east–west here (with the Chichester arm going roughly north). The original course east went across the road, through the farm buildings and on to Yapton and Ford, where it joined the River Arun.

Continue along the canal to Selsey Tramway Bridge. This old railway ran from 1897 to 1935 and carried both goods and passengers between Chichester and Selsey, which is a little over 6 miles to the south of here. The towpath continues to a road and Crosbie Bridge which was culverted in 1924/5. At the next road (Cutfield Bridge), the towpath changes banks. Just before entering the Chichester Yacht Basin, look left to the canal and the weir that marks the remains of the first sea lock, Manhood End Lock. Having pondered the origins of this name, continue along the road adjacent

A ketch negotiates The Hundred of Manhood & Selsey Tramway's lifting bridge at Hunston on the Chichester Canal in 1897

The Boat Museum Archive

to the canal basin. Here you will find a chandlery and a café-cum-bar which serves sandwiches and drinks. If you continue further along the remaining length of canal, you will pass a swing bridge named after Lord Egremont and then the final sea lock, Salter's Lock.

To return to Chichester, it is possible to devise a route which takes a signposted footpath across the entrance to the yacht basin and out alongside woodland and fields to New Barn. Bear left along a metalled lane to a road, turn right and then left along another lane to Apuldram. The road bends right past a manor house and then left. At the next left bend, there should be a public right of way across the field back into Chichester. When I was here, however, it was clear that walkers were not welcome and I was forced to continue along the road and on via a hazardous crossing of the bypass back to the railway station. This route is possible but frankly you would be better off relaxing in the bar for a bit longer and returning along the canal.

Further Information

The focus for all the activity along the W&A is of course the Canal Trust. It has undertaken clearance and dredging work, rebuilt locks and reconstructed bridges. The aim is not to rebuild the canal itself but to convince government at all levels of the feasibility of the project. It can be contacted via:

Mr J.R. Wood
24 Griffiths Avenue,
Lancing,
West Sussex BN15 0HW.

The Trust publishes a newsletter and a quarterly magazine. It also sells the Wey–South Path book.

The Chichester Canal has its own supporters who can be reached at:

The Chichester Canal Society,
Jaspers,
Coney Road,
East Wittering,
West Sussex PO20 8DA.

For detailed information on the history of all the waterways involved, the best reference is:

Vine, P.A.L., *London's Lost Route to the Sea*. David & Charles, 4th edition, 1986.

The Victorian guide to the canal is available in reprint:

Dashwood, J.B., *The Thames to the Solent by Canal and Sea*. Shepperton Swan, Shepperton, 1868, republished 1980.

APPENDICES

A: General Reading

This book can, of course, only provide you with a brief glimpse of the waterway network. Other authors are more qualified than me to fill the gaps and the following reading matter may help those who wish to know more.

Magazines

There are two monthly canal magazines that are available in most newsagents: *Canal & Riverboat* and *Waterways World*. Both have canal walks columns.

Books

There is a wide range of canal books available, varying between guides for specific waterways to learned historical texts. There should be something for everyone's level of interest, taste and ability to pay.

All the books listed here are available in paperback unless marked with an asterisk.

For a good introduction to canals that won't stretch the intellect, or the pocket, too far:

Smith, P.L., *Discovering Canals in Britain*. Shire Books, 1984.
Burton, A. and Platt, D., *Canal*. David & Charles, 1980.
Hadfield, C., *Waterways sights to see*. David & Charles, 1976.*
Rolt, L.T.C., *Narrowboat*. Methuen, 1944.
This can be taken a few steps further with the more learned:

Hadfield, C., *British Canals*. David & Charles, 1984; new edition, Alan Sutton, to be published 1993.

At least three companies publish boating guides:
Nicholson's Guides to the Waterways. Three volumes.
Pearson's Canal & River Companions. Eight volumes (so far).
Waterways World. Eight volumes (so far).

Readers seeking further walking books should look no further than:
Quinlan, Ray, *Canal Walks: Midlands*. Alan Sutton Publishing, 1992.
Quinlan, Ray, *Canal Walks: North*. Alan Sutton Publishing, to be published 1993.

B: Useful Addresses

British Waterways

BW is the guardian of the vast majority of the canal network and deserves our support. There are offices all over the country but the customer services department can be found at:

British Waterways,
Greycaine Road,
Watford,
WD2 4JR.
Tel: 0923-226422

Inland Waterways Association

The IWA was the first, and is still the premier, society that campaigns for Britain's waterways. It publishes a members' magazine, *Waterways*, and provides various services. There are numerous local groups which each hold meetings, outings, rallies, etc. Head office is at:

Inland Waterways Association,
114 Regent's Park Road,
London,
NW1 8UQ.
Tel: 071-5862556

Towpath Action Group

The Towpath Action Group campaigns for access to and maintenance of the towpaths of Britain and publishes a regular newsletter.

Towpath Action Group,
23 Hague Bar Road,
New Mills,
Stockport,
SK12 3AT.

C: Museums

A number of canal museums are springing up all over the country. The following are within reach of the area covered within this book and are wholly devoted to canals or have sections of interest:

THE NATIONAL WATERWAYS MUSEUM
Llanthony Warehouse,
Gloucester Docks,
Gloucester,
GL1 2EH.
Tel: 0452-307009

THE CANAL MUSEUM
Stoke Bruerne,
Towcester,
Northamptonshire,
NN12 7SE.
Tel: 0604-862229

THE NATIONAL MARITIME MUSEUM
Exeter Quay and Docks,
Haven Road,
Exeter,
EX2 8DT.
Tel: 0392-58075

INDEX

Arun Navigation 161–7, 173
Avon, River 84, 86, 87, 89, 92–4, 97
Avoncliff Aqueduct 91–3

Barnes, James 70–2
Basingstoke Canal vii, viii, 1–15, 168
Beeleigh 56, 58–9, 63–4, 66
Birmingham Canal Navigations 146, 150
Birmingham & Fazeley Canal 103–4
Birmingham & Liverpool Junction Canal 109
Blisworth 68, 71–2, 74
Braunston 68–9, 71–2, 74, 80–2, 100, 102, 105–7, 113
Brecon & Abergavenny Canal viii, 15–28
Bridgwater & Taunton Canal viii, 29–42, 148
Brindley, James 24, 100, 102, 109–10, 112, 146–7
Bristol & Taunton Canal 29–30
Bristol & Western Canal 30
Brown, John 132, 134
Brynich Aqueduct 22–4
Bude Canal viii, ix, 43–55

Caen Hill Locks 84, 87, 97–8
Cann Quarry Canal 39
Cartwright, Thomas 17
Chard Canal 32, 35–7, 39
Chelmer & Blackwater Navigation viii, 56–67
Chichester Canal 174–6
Claverton pumping station 85–6, 94
Commercial Canal 72
Coventry Canal 70, 100–4, 117
Crofton pumping station 84, 87, 98–9
Crossley, William 17
Croydon Canal 163
Crumlin branch 15–16

Dadford, John 17
Dadford, Thomas 16
Dadford, Thomas jun. 16–17, 22, 26

Dorset & Somerset Canal 39, 88
Dudley & Stourbridge Canal 146
Dundas Aqueduct 88, 93–4

Edyvean, John 44
Exeter Canal 29–31, 40–2

Fulton, John 45

Glamorganshire Canal 16, 83
Gloucester & Berkeley Canal 149
Gloucester & Hereford Canal ix
Gloucester & Sharpness Canal ix
Grand Junction Canal viii, ix, 68–83, 100, 105–7, 113, 116–8, 120, 126, 148–9
Grand Southern Canal 163
Grand Surrey Canal 3
Grand Union Canal 68–83, 106, 120–1
Grand Western Canal ix, 29–30, 32–4, 35, 39, 148
Green, James 40–1, 46
Greywell Tunnel 1–3, 6, 12–14

Hampshire & Berkshire Canal 3
Hampton Gay Canal 70, 77, 105
Harmsworth, Alec 4, 5, 11–12
Hawkesbury Junction 100, 102, 104, 113
Hertford Union Canal 116, 119
Heybridge Basin 56, 58–60, 64–5
Hollinworth, James 31–2
Hore, James 17, 58, 86

Iden Lock 130, 135–8, 140–1
Itchen Navigation 3, 164

Jessop, Josias 164
Jessop, William 2, 71–2

Kennet & Avon Canal viii, ix, 3–4, 29–30, 57, 84–99, 148–9, 168
Kennet, River 84, 86–8

Lee & Stort Navigation ix, 116, 119, 122

Leeds & Liverpool Canal viii
Leicester line 68, 70, 74–5, 77, 120–1
Limehouse Basin 116, 128
London & Birmingham Junction Canal 105
London & South-Western Canal 4
London & Western Canal 70, 77, 105, 148

Marhamchurch incline 43, 46, 48–9, 52
Monmouthshire & Brecon Canal 15–28
Monmouthshire Canal 16, 19–20
Morgan, James 117–18

Nash, John 117–18, 124
Newbold-on-Avon 102–3, 113–14
North Wilts Canal 145, 149–50

Old Union Canal 68, 70–2, 74, 120
Oxford Canal viii, ix, 68–70, 72, 75, 77, 81–2, 100–15, 117, 148

Paddington Basin 68, 72–3, 116–18, 127–8
Parrett, River 30–1, 33, 38
Pinkerton, John 2, 12
Portsmouth & Arundel Canal 166, 173–6
Portsmouth, Southampton & London Junction Canal 3, 164

Regent's Canal 72, 74–5, 116–30
Rennie, John 30, 58, 60, 72–3, 86–7, 94, 117, 132–4, 173
Rother, River 130, 132–3, 135, 138–40, 163
Royal Military Canal viii, ix, 130–144

Sapperton Tunnel 145, 147–8, 150–1, 157–9
Simcock, Samuel 102–3, 110
Smeaton, John 44, 58
Somerset Coal Canal ix, 88, 94

Staffs & Worcs Canal viii, 146–7, 150
Stoke Bruerne 68, 72–3, 82–3
Stover & Hackney Canal 39
Stratford-upon-Avon Canal 105
Stroudwater Navigation 57, 69, 145–6, 150–1
Surrey & Hampshire Canal 4

Taunton & Uphill Canal 30
Tavistock Canal 39
Telford, Thomas 24, 76, 109, 118
Thames, River ix, 2–3, 7, 68, 72, 84–6, 88, 97, 100–1, 104, 116, 145–7, 149–50, 165
Thames & Severn Canal 69, 104, 145–60
Thurston, E. Temple 103, 110–11, 157
Tone, River 30–4, 35, 38
Trent, River 68, 70
Trent & Mersey Canal viii, 101, 103, 147
Trew, John 40–1
Tring reservoirs 68, 76–80

Vignole, Charles 105

Warwick Canals 72, 75, 100, 105–7, 113, 120, 148
Western Junction Canal 79
Western Union Canal 79
Weston, Samuel 103
Wey & Arun Junction Canal viii, 161–76
Wey Navigation ix, 7, 161–7, 173
Weybridge, Woking & Aldershot Canal 4
Whitworth, Robert 72, 103, 146, 149
Wilts & Berks Canal ix, 79, 88–9, 145, 149–50
Woking, Aldershot & Basingstoke Canal 4

Yarranton, Andrew 57, 109
Yeoman, Thomas 58